As They Find a Way

As They Find a Way

A journey of various creative
Zimbabwean women

Wizzy Mangoma & Teurai Chanakira

To order additional copies of this book, contact:
Xlibris Corporation
1-888-795-4274
www.Xlibris.com
Orders@Xlibris.com
104265

Dedication:

Thank you God—my Creator and ultimate inspiration. Thank you dearest sister and friend, Wizzy Mangoma and all those who support and encourage me. I dedicate this book to my mother, Elizabeth Chanakira, who is now in her spirit form and to the countless Zimbabwean creative women who are brave enough to follow their hearts.

Teurai Chanakira

....

Many thanks to The Almighty for lighting my path at all times.

This book is dedicated to you my mother, my family and friends who always believe in me no matter how bizarre my ideas may seem to you. Michala Donkor my dearest friend who came out of a coma during the making of this book and gave me more strength to believe in the much greater power of living.

Thank you Teurai for also believing in me, for your work ethics, for being a dear young sister (I never had) and a true friend. And, thanks to all the creative Zimbabwean women in this book for taking time to share your experiences with the world.

Wizzy Mangoma

Editorial:

These days everybody wants to be involved in the booming Entertainment, Arts and Media Industry, but very few know where to start or what is required to get the Industry's attention. This is particularly so amongst Africans in the Creative Arts Industry as a profession in the Arts has not historically been regarded as a viable route to make a living. There are countless visionaries and creative people who will never be seen or heard of due to the lack of exposure, a polished product, the correct image and lack of the knowledge on how to market themselves effectively.

Women have voices and stories to tell. Many women have been through continuous struggle for their voices to be heard. When most people around the globe think of women, and in particular, an African woman, one of the things that comes to mind is, someone who is submissive or someone who cannot deliver.

The voices of men have always overshadowed women's voices in many aspects. Men have always told their stories while women stood by their side. Who else can tell their own stories of sweet music that can be sang with melodies from the depth of the heart none other than the African Women themselves? The world can hear those untold stories through all forms of creativity such as Fashion, Styling, Art, Literature, Music, Dance, Theater, Painting, Film, Photography, Craft, Culinary arts and much more.

A lot of creative women are emerging as they realize the significance of their dreams. The women you are about to read about will take you on a journey of their lives.

As we create, we build a home of comfort for our soul. A home which can be understood by many, only if we give them the chance to walk in our world.

"Choose to align yourself with people who are like-minded in their search for inspiration. Your life is simplified enormously when you don't have to defend yourself to anyone, and when you receive support rather than criticism." ~ Dr. Wayne Dye

Before you criticize someone's work, stop and think, remember that whatever you are criticising was done from the heart.

Treasures of a Woman

Woman, you have treasures
hidden in your soul.
A beautiful gift, a bright flower
in a human garden.
Woman, you are nurturing
A source of comfort to human nature
A home to return to after
the harshness of ungrateful masters
A pillar, a peaceful shade
under the burning heat
The weight of the world
Is on your shoulders
Woman, wear no mask
your beauty shines from within
Love your fellow women
When you smile, they smile
When you cry, they cry
When you laugh, they laugh
Keep loving . . .
The world needs LOVE from you.

By Wizzy Mangoma

Sakara Cee (Michelle Adams)

Quote of your choice:

"Once you decide, the universe conspires to make it happen" (Ralph Waldo Emerson)

Bio:

I was born in Harare, Zimbabwe. I'm the first-born child, grandchild and niece in the family so was very well loved in my early years (and still), and I have taken my musical talent from both sides of the family. I've been living in the UK for 14 years, and work as a singer; I also own my own business "Miss African Spirit Beauty Pageant" and am a single mother of two children aged 8½ and 7.

How were you as a child—was there anything outstanding about your personality?

I asked my mum to give me some info about this question and she said:

"You've always thrived on being "in charge" of your peers and the younger ones. When left in charge, parents could rest assured that all the children would be well-behaved and instructed correctly in whatever they were doing e.g. playing games, cleaning up, etc.

You were always singing all over the house." (In other words I was, and still am bossy).

"You've been singing since you were a toddler, I remember at two/three years old, you were singing the nursery rhyme "I hear fumba" (A shona and English mix supposed to be "I hear thunder") and between the ages of three and four, you were taught to sing the same song, Frère Jacques in French by your aunty". Recognizing the tune in nursery school class one morning, you were very upset when you heard the lyrics the nursery school teacher was using—it was Brother John in "English". When I picked you up after the school day had ended, I heard that you brought the whole lesson to a standstill and that Mrs Bent, the nursery school teacher, was told in no uncertain terms that the lyrics were wrong. Mrs Bent didn't argue and then directed you to teach the French lyrics to the rest of the class while she played the piano . . . and so it was that the whole nursery school class (who had no idea what they were singing) learnt the French version."

I had to laugh when I heard this, I've heard the story many times, but it shows me that I always was a singer, always in charge and always bossy.

My mum also recalled that between the ages of three and four, I had learnt the lyrics of all the songs on the "Grease Lightning" album (featuring Olivia Newton John and John Travolta) and sang them with feeling—e.g. "Hopelessly devoted to you". I still love that song and sing it if I go to Karaoke!

Do you remember when you first realized your talent?

I remember being about five years old, singing at the top of my lungs in the backyard on the swing and I realized that I could make my voice imitate the notes that were being sung. For notes I couldn't do, I practiced over and over until I could. For many afternoons after school and during the school holidays from then, until well into my teenage years, I'd spend a lot of time doing that . . . listening to the radio or some records, learning the lyrics and practicing. It was only when I was about 13 that I realized it was a talent for singing. Despite many years of writing poetry as a young child, at the age of 13 I wrote my first song while sitting on the floor in my dad's bedroom while he played the guitar. He had told me to bring my poetry, he'd get his guitar and we'd see if we could do a song. I was nervous, but it was then that I realized that I could write songs. It only took about an hour to write the song and my dad and I practiced it together for a while.

Who/what was your inspiration?

I had been writing poetry for years before, but my dad inspired me to put those words to music. I could see his eyes shining with pride and he encouraged me to write more songs and poems, which I have been doing ever since. Music has always been all around me. My mom and I used to have a 'secret' stash of poetry that I would often read through without her knowing. Her words were so powerful and passionate. I would often creep through her stuff to have a read-through. My family was always a talented family in many ways; I was inspired to follow my dreams by watching others follow theirs, while I was still young.

Was there anyone who noticed your special talent, did you get any moral support?

I've always had moral support from my family, I've been encouraged by my parents, my Godmother and my late Aunt Zara. I used to sing in the church choir. In my whole life, I've had a total of about two months' worth of voice training: the first one was with the famous Zimbabwean opera singer Lorna Kelly, who was convinced that I could make it big in opera. I wasn't interested in that at all, but she was very encouraging. I had to stop my lessons because I couldn't afford to keep taking them.

How did people react to you when they noticed you were different—were you understood?

I've never really noticed if there was a reaction of any kind, particularly in my family. Many of us in the family are musically or artistically talented, and I think it's just expected that we all have a talent of some kind, so I don't think my talent is looked upon as remarkable in any way. Of all the family and friends that I've grown up with and with whom I am still close, they just know 'me'; they know what I'm like.

Being Zimbabwean, what were/ are expectations towards you as a female artist/creative being?

I'm inclined to think that people don't really know what to expect. So many artists in Zimbabwe embrace different genres. We come from such different cultures with different interests, even though we're all from the same country. Artists such as myself, Chiwoniso Maraire, Rozalla Miller, Laygwan Sharkie, Zuwa and Metaphysics are all so different, yet all Zimbabwean.

What path did you take to follow your vision?

In order to follow my vision I have always entered competitions—in Zimbabwe and in the UK. I use social media a lot (Facebook, twitter, Reverbnation, Myspace) and have once been 'accused' of "guerrilla marketing" by one of my old friends and fellow musician, Herbert Schwamborn. I would take ANY GIG, paid or unpaid, regardless of distance initially, and now I sing for a function band almost every weekend.

I always give 100% when I am on stage, and in fact my job starts from when I arrive at the venue. Even when I am ill or not "in the mood" I still sing like I mean it because that's what I'm getting paid to do. I try to keep it professional by answering all emails/phone calls, turning up on time and giving my best.

What is it that you would like to accomplish (for yourself or anyone) with your creative talent?

At the moment singing is my livelihood, I'd like to continue this work as I enjoy it so much, but I'd like to have much more focus on my original songs and go on regular tours bringing my music and talent to the world. I haven't been to Zimbabwe for about 12 years, so I'd love to do my first tour there and in as many African countries as I can manage. Of course this all needs music, so I am working on my first album at the moment (so far all I have released is singles).

I would like to be singing live and recording new songs for the rest of my life, the stage is where I want to always be.

What do you think could be done to empower creative children (in Zimbabwe)?

In my opinion, the most important things anyone can have are hope and freedom. Children everywhere *must* have a dream. I think it's important not to swat a child's attempts to create; we must seek their strengths; help them to develop those strengths and we must be honest with them about their ability, but be kind (if necessary). To start with, a belief that nothing is impossible would help, instead of restricting them to perceived ceilings and frowning of their attempts to fly. I think once anyone believes they can do something and they believe nothing is impossible, and then they are in possession of what they need to succeed.

What message do you have for creative women who feel they have no one to turn to?

Your strength comes from within. Nobody or no one circumstance can dictate what you achieve in any area of your life. Dare to dream of the "impossible". Dare to make it happen and work towards it bit by bit, day by day.

Currently, I live on a very poor estate in Milton Keynes. I am a single mom of two, I have hardly any family around to help or support and I have even fewer friends nearby. Yet I still manage. I have minimal income and drive a car that really is overdue to replace/repair, but my children and I are happy and still I follow my dreams. I believe that one day I will have whatever I want. I run a business in a situation where I'm never certain where I'm going to get the money from, but I still dare to dream of the kind of business I want. And still I manage. I practice daily to visualize my dreams, to plan and move in the direction of the success that I dare to imagine. Life is short; my belief is that I need to do everything that I can do before my borrowed time runs out.

The advice I would give to any creative woman who has no one to turn to is, *turn to your creativity.* Work through that and from that your best work may come. Maybe the fact that you don't have anyone to turn to is a lesson in self-sufficiency and personal strength. Embrace it as just another experience and ride the storm. Nothing lasts, not even grief. Look for the future day when you will have what you want, picture it, dare to dream.

Sympathy Ngwenya Sibanda

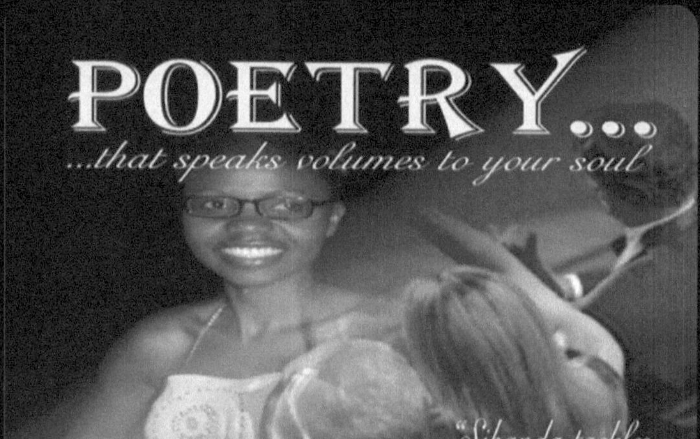

Bio:

Sympathy Ngwenya Sibanda is a writer who has published an anthology titled, "Matters of Life" in 2009, with an audio version coming soon.

She owns a Poetry Consultancy called "Dunamis", which offers poetry performances at weddings, other special occasions, trains upcoming public speakers and links them with other established performers.

She liaises with "Daffodils Gifts", a company that designs personalized anytime and occasional cards by providing relevant poems.

Sympathy is also an advocate for women and children's rights.

Favourite quote:

"Womanhood is a matter of celebration; I'm here to make an impression".

How were you as a child—was there anything outstanding about your personality?

I was an extrovert and used to interact with people who were much older than me. People used to marvel at how inquisitive I was, I used to thirst for more and more information and hence I was a bookworm. My toys as a baby were not dolls or cooking pots, but books—Discovery, Adventure and Bible stories. When asked to recite what I would have read, I would regurgitate everything as it was.

Do you remember when you first realized your talent?

My parents inculcated the idea that I was an exceptional child at an early age, so I just grew up knowing I had a special gift.

Who/what was your inspiration

There are several people who inspired me. Of special mention are my parents, who have always shown enthusiasm towards my capabilities and my primary teacher Mrs. Gondongwe, who was my childhood role model. On the other hand, life has always been and continues to be my inspiration because there are so many lessons that we draw from experiences we go through every second of the day.

Was there anyone who noticed your special talent, 'did you get any moral support?

Oh yes! 'Nerds' are always noticed. My church leader brother, Nathan Madhembe, afforded opportunities to my friends and I to speak to very large and heterogeneous congregations. This boosted my self-esteem as I noticed how we would impact on these people. I was so blessed to have very supportive people around me from the time I was young because all my teachers understood me and would alert me when there was a competition that would help.

How did people react to you when they noticed you were different-were you understood?

I have realized that everyone would want to be associated with a clever young girl or boy, such was my privilege. I was very fortunate to belong to the church that I go to because peculiarity is actually encouraged than discouraged, therefore I received support that acted as a catalyst to even better things.

Being Zimbabwean, what were/ are expectations towards you as a female artist/creative being?

I believe in equal opportunities in spite of one's gender, every gate should be open for me to enter and shouldn't be closed just because I am a woman. As Zimbabweans, we are getting there and that is pleasing. As a Zimbabwean and more so a woman, I am here to make an impression!

What path did you take to follow your vision?

There is a quote that I love which says, "We miss opportunities because they come wearing overalls"— industriousness, networking and persistence helped me realize my dream. I always had a friendship with all my Languages teachers, who in turn would inform me about any competition or organization that I should join in order to excel in my field. I joined the Budding Writers Association of Zimbabwe, Girl Child Network and many writing clubs. To all other artists, my advice is, hang around with people who will help you, networking helps and acquire the necessary qualifications because we are in a global village where competition is rife and you have to really strive to keep afloat.

What is it that you would like to accomplish (for yourself or anyone) with your creative talent?

I specialize in propagating love, peace and happiness. All I wish to do is make other people realize that life is worth celebrating against all odds and learn to make the best of their relationships.

What do you think could be done to empower creative children in Zimbabwe?

Parents should be encouraged to have time with their children and encourage them in areas of their talents. Similarly, organizations, the corporate world in conjunction with schools, should conduct competitions and career guidance that help empower children in realizing themselves. Schools should have programmes for children where they invite their role models from various sectors in order to "catch them young."

What message do you have for creative women who feel they have no one to turn to?

When you think the world is falling apart—open your eyes and you will realize that there are so many people and organizations you can turn to. So many established artists are willing to help you, what you have to do is take the first step.

Email: *sympathysibanda@yahoo.com*

Facebook: 'Sympathy Ngwenya Sibanda'

Black Bird

Quote:

"Live your best Life . . ." (Oprah Winfrey)

Bio:

I was born in 1983 at Mbuya Nehanda Maternity Hospital in Harare, to a Zambian mother and a South African father. My mixed origin allowed for so much variety growing up and as a result I speak seven languages. My upbringing was split between Zimbabwe and South Africa. I am the last born in a family of two boys and two girls. Being the last of my mother's four children made me a real mommy's baby, making it really difficult for me when she died in 1995. I was only 11 years old and because my parents had separated, I spent two years in the Harare Children's Home.

After completing high school in Johannesburg, I went on to study Film in college and was married three years later in 2005. After having two children in the marriage, we got a divorce in 2008 and I have been a single mother since. Despite the challenges of single parenthood I love my daughters—Minana (five years old) and Nia (three and a half years old).The pain I have faced is diluted by the joy of watching my beautiful girls growing in beauty and wisdom.

How were you as a child, anything outstanding about your personality?

I remember how everyone used to complain that I talk too much. I really was a *rap-a-span* type of child and I attracted many nicknames (including "Cheeky Chops") as a result. I was full of confidence and I said what was on my mind at every given opportunity. I was also a natural leader, a gifted storyteller and whenever other children were gathered; I was either telling them one of my enthralling tales or giving instructions on who was playing what game next.

It's really funny though because right now I'm facing a serious dilemma with my youngest child Nia. She loves to talk and when she isn't telling some story or other, she is singing. Sometimes it gets really annoying and every now and then I can be caught pleading for a moment of silence. Now I know what my mom went through.

Do you remember when you first realized your talent?

My earliest memory of being a musician was when I was about five or six years old. I composed (in my head because I couldn't write) a song called, "Are You Lost Girly" about a little girl who had no place to call home. The girl was cold, lonely and hungry and in the song I assure her that she will one day find a home. I remember singing my song day and night for weeks on end and it drove my whole family crazy. However, soon enough they all knew the words and even until today, they remember my first hit single.

Another similar moment occurred in Grade One when I performed in a play at Admiral Tait Primary School. I enjoyed every second of being the narrator in "The Ginger Breadman" and the thrill of being on stage that once, was enough to get me hooked onto the Performing Arts.

Was there anyone who noticed your talent, did you get any moral support?

When I was a child, my family was excited about my talent and I constantly won public speaking competitions and got cast in school plays. However as I grew older, I started to face more resistance and by the time I reached high school it was clear that my family weren't really keen on me becoming a performer.

However, as a child, there were two people who really nurtured my talent and helped me to develop it from a very young age. The first was Mrs. Pollock (my Speech and Drama teacher), she helped me to bring out

the gem that was within me and under her guidance, I entered and won several Allied Arts competitions during Grade One and Two.

The second person who saw my talent at an early age was one of our childhood neighbours, Mr. Mike Hundu. He was a Sound Engineer at Media Associates in Rhodesville and from as young as six years old, I was being called to the studio to record voiceovers for radio and TV advertisements. During these years, I did several advertising campaigns including 'bubble gummers' and so many popular adverts. Those were my first jobs and as a part-time voiceover artist, I had a decent amount of pocket money to keep my bank balance healthy.

How did people react to you when they noticed you were different, were you understood?

According to my family, I was too clever to waste myself on the Arts. Throughout my school years I excelled academically and they felt that someone of my 'intelligence' should be a doctor, an architect or a pilot. I think that in their minds they couldn't understand my decision to walk away from the opportunity to makes lots of money in a well paid job and choose to go on the uncertain path of becoming a professional rapper. When I was young they thought it was a passing phase, but as

I grew older I became more and more distant from those close to me because they couldn't understand why it was important that I followed this path. Luckily things have improved. These days, I think they get the picture and it's clear that I am serious about being a Hip Hop artist.

Being Zimbabwean, what were/ are expectations towards you as a female artist/creative being?

Most of the challenges that I face as a female artist are based on false perceptions and stereotypes. As a female working in a male-dominated industry, I often spend most of my time with a bunch of guys and this makes some people uncomfortable. In their heads I must be morally loose and sleeping with the whole lot of them to be able to spend so much time with six or seven guys.

Another expectation that I found is in relation to my work hours and venues. As a musician, I often perform in nightclubs and bars, with my shows sometimes ending as late as 3am in the morning. To some people it is unacceptable that a lady be found in a bar unless she is the promiscuous type or a prostitute who is out looking for customers. Also in the conservative culture that is Zimbabwe, women are generally home by 6pm. For me, it's the exact opposite because I usually make supper

early so that when the kids come from pre-school, they have supper, take a bath and go to bed before I leave for work (often around 9 or 10pm). To my neighbours and relatives, this can be a bit weird because a woman is expected to be at home once the sun goes down and I do the exact opposite of that on a regular. Even with a babysitter on call, a lot of people seem to think a mother shouldn't be out at night. If you are, then it is concluded that you are indecent and you have no real morals in place.

What path did you take to follow your vision?

Over the past few years, the word 'Google' has become one of my favourite words and I have become a firm believer that you can find out virtually everything online. I have found that 'googling' can help you solve anything, all the way from career advice to health concerns. I often use Google to find out how to enhance my brand and I also watch the international music trends online to see what direction to take in terms of marketing, distribution etc. I also use the internet to keep up with all of the local newspapers and this allows me to keep abreast of what is happening on the local music scene.

I know that what is online is not always fact as it is uploaded by various individuals, but I balance the information I get from various web pages with any other existing information that I might have. By using the most of technology to supplement your knowledge of your craft, an artist can expose themselves to a kaleidoscope of ideas which one can tailor to suit one's individual needs.

What is it that you would like to accomplish (for yourself or anyone) with your creative talent?

I want Black Bird to go down in the history books for being the first female African rapper to break several records within the sphere of music production as performance. As it stands, I recently made history at HIFA (Harare International Festival of the Arts) during April 2011 of the festival, when I became the first female Hip Hop artist to ever be invited to perform at the prestigious festival. For me, this is just the beginning because I have a lot up my sleeve and I have set really high standards for myself.

Rappers are generally considered to be uncouth and rowdy youths who possess no admirable qualities. I want to prove that this stereotype is wrong and I already have begun on my path to redeeming the powerful genre that is Hip-Hop music. I cannot say too much right now, but people can look out for a Guinness World Record and

a Grammy Award from Black Bird within the next few years.

What do you think can be done to empower creative children in Zimbabwe?

I think that the greatest empowerment a creative child can receive is to have supportive and open-minded parents. Most artists never achieve their full potential because their families and society in general, often discourage their advancement in their art. To place some focus on helping parents and families of creatives, would benefit creative children because their parents will be equipped with the knowledge to nurture their children's gifting, making success even more achievable because of the existence of a strong support system. Creating support groups for such parents and families can give them a chance to interact with other creative children's parents and as a group; they can find solutions to any psychological obstacles and fears, which they may be facing.

What message do you have for creative women who feel alone?

The best advice I can give to creative women is that they should come out of their shells and seek out events, associations and even online groups and chat rooms that are created by and for women in the Arts.

Most countries have a National Arts body and they can be very useful in guiding you to other women who are in your field and geographic location. Having regular contact with other female artists can help you see that you aren't alone and you can get ideas on how to overcome your challenges from women who are facing similar problems in their own communities. You are never alone, you just have to go out there and find other women who are doing what you do and more often than not, they can turn out to be a real source of strength and encouragement.

Reading books like this and the biographies of successful women in the Arts can also give you that extra boost to keep going.

Tsitsi Mutendi

Quote of your choice:

"I am here for a purpose & that purpose is to grow into a mountain and not shrink to a grain of sand. Henceforth I will apply all my efforts to become the highest mountain of all and I will strain my potential until it cries for mercy." (Og Mandino)

This is my daily mantra. I live and breathe it.

Bio:

Tsitsi Mutendi is the driving force behind DanTs Media in her dual role as Managing Director of the company and Founding Editor of *JEWEL* Magazine. Tsitsi holds a Bachelor of Commerce Degree in Marketing.

From 2009 to date, Tsitsi has been the Founding president of NGO Women of Legacy Foundation (WOLF) which has led to her being featured in various media and publications for her inspirational work. From its inception, she has managed to successfully run two multinational conferences with audiences of influential women from across the continent and its various Diaspora. WOLF currently has a membership database which includes the Who's Who of women in various industries, civil society and governments across Africa.

Tsitsi is also an established Fashion Designer with two distinct and popular labels, namely, **Totem**, African Couture and **Kimberly M** Maison Couture. Kimberly M is an upscale women's fashion design house. The label is all about femininity, glamour, high drama and luxurious fabrics. Sultriness, sensuality, distinction, chic and elegance influence the trademarks of this brand—tailored chic at its best.

Totem is a chic African wear label that creates garments for the modern day African Woman. The garments are all made from or include JAVA/ANKARA in their design and creation—African fabrics cut and styled in creative modern trendy styles. Think shift dresses, pencil skirts, trench coats, shirts etc in African prints mixed with satins, silks, denims etc.

How were you as a child—was there anything outstanding about your personality?

I was very creative—I studied Art, played the violin throughout primary school and made numerous wardrobes for my dolls. I was also very observant, free willed (my mother can attest to this) and spiritual (I remember as a child being able to empathise and always trying to understand situations and people).

Do you remember when you first realized your talent?

When I was in primary school I was creative but took it for granted, as every child may do growing up. When

I was in high school however, I realized I was a bit different because I wanted more. I knew there was more to life than the traditional route of school, job, marriage, kids, and death. I wanted to do more, be more, see more and I wanted this for others. A lot of people didn't understand that about me.

Who/what was your inspiration?

My mom and Literature. I am an avid reader, particularly of magazines. Growing up, I wanted to live out what I saw in the pages of my books and magazines. I wanted to one day achieve what these other people were achieving. I wanted to create what I read and saw. My mom taught me that I could do anything and always found ways of allowing me to express and explore my creativity whilst cheering me on.

Was there anyone who noticed your special talent, did you get any moral support?

My mom and my husband. I met my husband 12 years ago and we got married two years ago. From the time that I met him when I was in Form 2, he always used to tell me I was very talented and special. My mom has been saying the same to me all my life. That goes a long way, particularly when you want to give up.

How did people react to you when they noticed you were different—were you understood?

A lot of the time people dismissed me as just a dreamer who had her head lost in the clouds. That may be true to some, but I have learnt that most great people of any time have had such said about them. It is good to dream. Nothing can be achieved if you don't dream. Always see the bigger picture—your bigger picture.

Being Zimbabwean, what were/ are expectations towards you as a female artist/creative being?

I like to see myself as a Creative Artist. I like to create beautiful things, meaningful things, lasting legacies. As a Creative Female Artist in Zimbabwe, people expect you to give up easily, go back to the kitchen and do what women "do". They expect you to do things for free and sometimes undervalue your work and your talent. The best way to put it, is that you are not taken as seriously as the male artists, therefore you have to work twice as hard to prove yourself and you have to prove that what your passion is, is not a whim; but a career, income earner, economy builder and culture influencer.

Another issue is that in Zimbabwe a lot of the influential positions are held by men and as artists when you approach them with a proposal, they don't take you seriously and instead they start thinking sinister thoughts which include, "lunches" "after-hour meetings" etc. This degrades female artists; some fall prey to such shenanigans and lose their way. If it doesn't grow you as an artist and it erodes you as a person, walk away. There are other ways to grow.

What path did you take to follow your vision?

As a Marketer, I could share various ways in which artists can market themselves but this is not Marketing 101. Each artist wants to reach a certain type of audience and therefore must research on which is the best way to reach them. Being an artist doesn't mean you are a hobo who lives off the land. Learn to be business savvy. If you wisen up, you will create enough money to sustain yourself and your creativity while living comfortably.

Here is my path:

A) I first envisioned where I wanted to go—the bigger picture. If you can see the end, then you know where best to begin. The pathway in the middle is a learning curve that prepares you for your goal. As you grow, so will the picture and the end evolve.

B) I learnt from the best. The world is full of mentors from all walks of life. I benchmark my goals against those people who inspire me.

C) I got an educational qualification that was multifunctional and helpful to my creativity.

D) I surrounded myself with cheerleaders.

E) I learnt that no matter how many times I fall, its just another opportunity to get up again (smarter than before).

F) NEVER GIVE UP.

What is it that you would like to accomplish/ have accomplished (for yourself or anyone) with your creative talent?

I am only just beginning. I have amazing things that I am still left to do. I would like to put Zimbabwe on the international fashion map. I would like to get African women on a legacy-building journey that will influence their sisters the world over. I would like to celebrate JEWEL's 50th birthday. I would like to inspire my little girls. Most importantly, I want to become the highest mountain of all, exploring all that God has placed in me and using it to His glory.

What do you think could be done to empower creative children (in Zimbabwe)?

Nurturing. Parents in Zimbabwe see their children taking the traditional route, the traditional careers such as doctors, nurses, teachers, lawyers and accountants—jobs that they believe will feed them. This mindset should be changed. Children should be nurtured through creative camps, groups at school etc. Let the children follow their God-given talent. If God gave them the talent, He knew how He would provide for them. God is the only provider no matter how hard we try.

What message do you have for creative women who feel they have no one to turn to?

BELIEVE: in yourself, in your talent, in God.

Pat Brickhill

How were you as a child—was there anything outstanding about your personality?

I was a reserved child—and although I spent a happy childhood and come from a large family and extended family, I lived largely in my imagination. My imagination was always my constant companion.

Do you remember when you first realized your talent?

I have always enjoyed writing—but lacked confidence and self belief.

I did a writing course in Harare in the 90's with an amazing bunch of women and it was there that I realized there was a key to unlocking the talent that lies within and that I had talent!

Who/what was your inspiration?

Life has been my inspiration—giving birth made me aware that I was capable of creating beauty. Reading my favourite writers, as a child: Enid Blyton, Laura Lee Hope, Mark Twain, and later; Neville Shute, Graham Greene, Ngugi Wa Thiongo, Margaret Atwood, Dambudzo Marechera, Yvonne Vera, Stanley Nyamfukuza, John le Carre, Shimmer Chinodya, Barbara Kingsolver and Chimamanda Ngozi Adichie and others, has always been an inspiration and a comfort.

Irene Staunton is an amazing and inspiring Editor—Zimbabwe's finest.

Was there anyone who noticed your special talent, where did you get any moral support?

No teacher at school ever identified any talent for writing—I was often too far off-centre I think. People sometimes admired my letter writing—but generally I just knew I had to write. As an adult, I worked with John Gaetsewe, General Secretary of SACTU, who encouraged me to write speeches and articles for him.

I have always kept notebooks where I have written my thoughts, created stories and started many, many 'books'. My writing was always where I escaped to when I was sad, unhappy or joyful.

Moral support has always come from my children: Tomas, Liam and Amy; Joe; Tom and Anthony; Michael and Zolii and the amazing women in my life—Amy, Spike, Harriet, Zolii, Joyce, Anna, Heather, Esi, Mary, Muffet, Liz, Miriam, Joan amongst others.

How did people react to you when they noticed you were different—were you understood?

I have never been truly understood—except by myself!! We all yearn to belong, to fit in. Sometimes I have felt very isolated from others—almost shunned at school, painfully shy at times. I have only come into my own—celebrating my difference, as I have gotten older.

Being Zimbabwean, what were/ are expectations towards you as a female artist/creative being?

Being Zimbabwean taught me that there are always stones and other obstacles on the path. We have to keep striving. Women in Zimbabwe are competing in an essentially traditional male world where there is pressure to conform to a stereotype.

But being Zimbabwean taught me that we must 'to thine own self be true' and be prepared to stand alone.

What path did you take to follow your vision?

The first step on the path is to write, write, write—everyday—even when you are tired, busy, uninspired—writing must become like breathing, like food and water.

I learned that doing a writing course where we were encouraged to find the inner confidence to allow oneself to be vulnerable and exposed can open the door. In my case Aileen Hoffman was an amazing facilitator.

Most of all, you need to develop a benchmark of knowing your writing. Friends who read your writing offer a reflection, which is important in order to become objective (as opposed to subjective), about your writing.

Believe in yourself. The clichéd advice NOT to get discouraged is also important. If you want to get published, remember that you might need to draft and redraft many times, polish, edit. You will need to set things aside to let them rest, to maintain perspective. Be prepared for rejection letters—many now famous authors were rejected, 10, 20, 30 or more times!

What is it that you would like to accomplish/ have accomplished (for yourself or anyone) with your creative talent?

My dream is to live through my writing. Being recognized in Zimbabwe, the place I love is also of paramount importance to me. I hope to become more widely published . . . to keep writing all the stories that live within me.

What do you think could be done to empower creative children (in Zimbabwe)?

Children need to have books to read. Creative children need to be able to appreciate the joy of transferring thoughts and ideas to words. Writing is therapeutic; it is a friend when you are lonely, a blanket when you are cold, a memory of both joy and sadness.

Because of the economic woes, books—and therefore writing—have been pushed further away from priorities. Perhaps some incentives to creative young people, such as prizes, can help give access to the tools of the trade—dictionaries, other creative writing, pen, paper and computers.

What message do you have for creative women who feel they have no one to turn to?

We are thousands of creative women who might feel isolated and lonely—but that's only because we don't know each other. We are like a family who only need to meet—sharing our stories in one way—so write, write, write—don't give up!

Sharon "Shaniqua" Makombeshamu

Sharon Mombeshamu
by Claudia Sangiorgi Dalimore

Quote of your choice:

Well it's hard to pin it down to one so I'll share a little something I like to call the 'trio of wisdom'. "Life is what you make it. Time is money that never returns. If others can do it, why can't I?" (Alice Chitauro—my grandmother's words of wisdom).

Bio:

Sharon "Shaniqua" Makombeshamu is the force behind Up and Coming Solo Artist Quashani Bahd™. Born in the heart of Southern Africa, Zimbabwe, at the age of 19, she packed up her suitcase and bade her family farewell to travel to "the land Down Under" to study. Embracing Melbourne's culture and its diversity, she now calls Melbourne home.

Quashani Bahd coins her genre of music, "Regglues", as "poetic, sweet melodies infused with life experiences, struggles, celebrations, hopes, dreams and passion for reggae and adoration for the blues". Quashani Bahd has featured her solo work onstage with local Melbourne Acts Elemente, Jabula, Ras JahKnow Band and Kundalila. Quashani Bahd's strong sense of community has also meant that she has had the privilege to be a part of Oxfam's Concert for Refugees 2010, Hope for Uganda 2010, and Sisters for Sisters 2011. Quashani Bahd also debuted with Dub Vyze Sound at the inaugural and acclaimed Oz Soul'Collective.

Quashani Bahd has also previously worked with a variety of Melbourne based Producers, to name a few, Gangsta Shadow 2004-2005 and Nyasha Hama (France) 2004. Quashani has featured on tracks such as "Roses" 2005 & 'So Addicted' 2009 for JL—Michael Lang (AUS) and "The Name is Shoc-Facta" 2004 for Shoc-Facta (UK).

Quashani has had much success on Reverbnation with her hit singles, "Georgey Porgey" & "Mista Self Important", which entered the charts at number 15 on 25April 2010 and then climbed into the Top Five. Quashani's up and coming album, "Born to Shine", will show case a variety of songs from various genres: Reggae, Dancehall, Jazz, Blues, Neo soul and Rhythm & Blues. The album is currently in production. A launch date is yet to be scheduled.

In addition to her solo pursuits, Quashani Bahd's passion for music has her involved in a number of other music groups: Melbourne outfit Kundalila (Acoustic /Acapella), Dub Vyze Sound (Reggae/ Dancehall), Ras JahKnow Band (Reggae), Jabula (African Choir) and Advent (Gospel Choir).

Her creative pursuits also extend to fashion, particularly accessory design. She is the creative force behind the bold creations from the House of BohoChic by Quashani.

'Bold' is one word for describing her creations. Colourful, chic, charming, bohemian and trendy are others, to mention a few. Her body of work really speaks for itself—from brightly coloured, hand cut, felt, bold feathers, fancy buttons to lace trims, gypsy frills, organza and satin flare. They all create textures and layers of visual appreciation for the modern day groovy chick.

The House of BohoChic has a wide offering of stylish accessories from button bracelets, satin necklaces, beaded necklaces, feather & felt trim rings, but is mostly adored for its' Fascinators. All creations are hand-custom made to suit individual tastes.

Sharon says her creations are a medium through which she shares the gift of her creative and expressive talent with women that appreciate boldness. Her Spring Carnivale 2010 Collection was launched on June 17, 2010.

How were you as a child—was there anything outstanding about your personality?

I wouldn't say there was anything outstanding about my personality as a child, but I have always been confident. In primary school, I loved Public Speaking.

Do you remember when you first realized your talent?

I always loved to sing from a very young age. The fondest memory I have is my first performance in Grade Five at the age of ten for a Class Talent Show. I sang two songs: "the Shoop Shoop Song (It's in His Kiss)", a song written by Rudy Clark which became a hit when it was recorded by Betty Everett. The second song was Jimmy Clanton's "Venus in Blue Jeans".

Who/what was your inspiration?

Inspiration is all around us. For instance, it is in our experiences, lessons learnt, our struggles, dreams, hopes, aspirations and nature. I draw my inspiration from life as I live it.

Was there anyone who noticed your special talent, did you get any moral support?

My creative talents were always evident from a very young age. I have been blessed to have supportive family and friends. Their support has been crucial to my journey as I pursue my creative passions.

How did people react to you when they noticed you were different—were you understood?

I have never been the sort of person that seeks other people's acceptance. I never strive to be understood.

Being Zimbabwean, what were/ are expectations towards you as a female artist/creative being?

I live in Melbourne—the melting pot of diverse cultures. I wouldn't say that there have been, or are expectations towards me as a female artist because of my background. If anything, I've always felt like the socio-cultural environment is accepting of artists from different backgrounds.

What path did you take to follow your vision?

It's probably good to stress that self-belief, motivation and above all, determination, are critical ingredients to successfully fulfill one's vision. Everyone's journey is different. We all have different strengths and weaknesses. It'd be a good start to note these and then work on strengthening the weaknesses depending on your craft. This is essential for one's growth. I am still on my journey. I think what has been helpful for me is being open-minded and being keen to meet new people. After all, opportunities arise from meeting new people and sharing your vision and passion with them.

The journey of an artist can be a challenging one. Sometimes not everyone is going to be supportive of your pursuit and it might take a little longer for you to attain certain goals you've set, so it's good to be patient and to stay determined.

What is it that you would like to accomplish/ have accomplished (for yourself or anyone) with your creative talent?

I would love to share my experiences with my audiences and ultimately empower women everywhere. I would love to give back to the community.

What do you think could be done to empower creative children (in Zimbabwe)?

Firstly, before empowering creativity in children, I strongly feel it is of paramount importance that creativity in children be nurtured early in their learning. Adding creative components to the learning curriculum in schools could do this. Exposing creativity to children in visual, literary and performing arts would foster creativity from a very young age. However, to empower them would entail support from their family and the community.

What message do you have for creative women who feel they have no one to turn to?

Creativity is a form of expressing oneself. Being creative in itself can be quite healing. I would encourage them to pursue and indulge in their creative passion.

www.facebook.com/houseofbohochicbyquashani

www.reverbnation.com/quashanibahd

www.kundalila.com

Tsitsi Muchenje Nyabako

Quote :

"There's always hope as long as you are alive." (Author unknown)

Bio:

I was born in Harare, Zimbabwe on August 16 1982. I'm a fashion model whose career has grown over the past eight years. I have participated in several fashion shows, including the Virtues & Vices Show in Toronto. I have also worked with some amazing Fashion Designers over the years.

My career started in 2002 after a photographer said he thought I had potential in the modeling industry & advised me to do a photo shoot to begin with. I followed his advice and the pictures were amazing. I immediately enrolled in modeling school at the Barbizon School of Modeling in Dallas, Texas and soon after I started competing in local pageants. My first pageant was the Face of Zimbabwe in which I was chosen as 2nd Princess.

After moving to Toronto, I signed myself up with a modeling agency and my career took off. From there I participated in several other fashion shows, including-The Clothing Show Spring & Fall Collections 2008-2009, Fantasy Fashion Showcase and Estella Couture Fashion. Furthermore, I appeared in Lou Lou Magazine, worked with MTV Canada and was in the Agua Del Pozo music video.

How were you as a child—was there anything outstanding about your personality?

As a child I was very energetic. I'm the only girl in our family and have two younger brothers, so I'd always try to keep up with them whether it was at sports, in school or at home. I was very competitive and that led me to be a star athlete in high school.

Do you remember when you first realized your talent?

I first realized my talent when I took part in my first pageant & won Second Princess in the Face of Zimbabwe pageant. I felt very confident and loved the energy that surrounds the stage. From then on, I knew modeling was something I loved & would pursue.

Who/what was your inspiration?

My mom inspired me & continues to do so. She always used to dress up and wear perfume when she left the house to go to work. That would boost her confidence and wherever she was, she would light up the room. She would always make me feel beautiful in and out and I'd be so proud walking next to her.

Was there anyone who noticed your special talent, did you get any moral support?

Yes, a photographer called Terence, noticed my special talent and encouraged me to do my first photo shoot. My family and friends were very supportive of my talent and suggested I take it further, so I then enrolled in modeling school so that I could learn the basics of being a model.

How did people react to you when they noticed you were different—were you understood?

At first I would say I was misunderstood when people saw I was dressing differently and that I was a model. Maybe they thought I had lost my way by taking up such a career, but I kept my head up and continued pursuing my talent. My family also helped me through with the moral support they gave me.

Being Zimbabwean, what were/ are expectations towards you as a female artist/creative being?

I would say the expectation is to put Zimbabwe on the map in the industry. There is so much talent in Zimbabwe and around the world. However, there are so many artists trying to break into the industry, it's a lot of work just to make it through.

What path did you take to follow your vision?

The path I took is a good start for aspiring models. Take modeling lessons, whether it's from a modeling class or from another model. Get the basics: how to walk on the runway, how to pose for photos, how to apply make up/skin care, how to dress up for different occasions and fashion essentials that you must have in your closet. It would be good to learn basic acting skills too, so that you have options to further your career. Then buy a good portfolio for your pictures. Next, you must do a photo shoot with different poses and fashion looks (business, casual and fashion). From this shoot, make sure you get headshots & full body shots, so you can have a variety in your portfolio. The next step would be to research online & find a reputable modeling agency as they will be the ones to get you work by sending you to auditions & casting calls. They will get you to do more photo shoots to update your portfolio and provide you with comp cards, which have your measurements & contact information. It's also good to join sites like **www.modelmayhem. com** & create model profiles on **www.facebook.com** to network and look for auditions.

What is it that you would like to accomplish/ have accomplished (for yourself or anyone) with your creative talent?

As a model, I would love to accomplish Supermodel status & be recognised around the world for being a Zimbabwean model making it in the industry. If not for me, then for any other Zimbabwean model, because we have so many beautiful people, with so much talent.

What do you think could be done to empower creative children (in Zimbabwe)?

I would say for the ones who are into the Fashion & Acting industries, having access to different affordable resources like modeling & acting schools in Zimbabwe would make an impact on empowering creative children. They learn so much about confidence & commanding the stage in such schools, thus it would go a long way in their lives.

What message do you have for creative women who feel they have no one to turn to?

When you realise your talent, never give up on it no matter what odds are against you. Surround yourself with family and friends that support your talent, as they will help you through the tough days. Do research on the Internet, from agencies or schools that are in your area which help you identify what your talent is and enroll yourself there. Teachers & professors can also be a good source for support & information.

You can also join clubs that focus on your talent, as they are a good place to learn and network. The more you learn about your talent, the better you become at it.

Rutendo Denise Mutsamwira
RuTendo DeNise (.R.)

Quote of your choice:

"To know your talent/gift/purpose on earth and not use it to your fullest potential is a mockery to your Creator". (Rutendo Denise Mutsamwira) (.R.)

Bio:

Rutendo Denise is 23 years old and a Final Year Student at MONASH University, South Africa. She is also Monash University South Africa's Student Association's Media Liaison, a Poet and aspiring Writer/Actress.

She has also started *#Knowurzimbos* on Twitter, a 140-character based networking group for Zimbabweans on Twitter, which she will later turn into a blog, as an online database.

How you were as a child—was there anything outstanding about your personality?

I was very loud! yet, bubbly and friendly. I was also very active in extra—curricular activities. I played marimba and was in the drama club all throughout high school.

Do you remember when you first realized your talent?

It was in 2005, when I was in Lower Six at Chisipite Senior School. I had written an essay in one of our Literature classes, it was read out to the class, and that's when I realised there was something there. However, I chose to live in denial for a long time about my talents. Even now, I get extremely shy and "awkwardly uncomfortable" when people compliment me for my work.

Who/what was your inspiration?

I draw inspiration from so many things: situations, relationships and interpretations. My inspiration has been my mother who was a teacher. I think my biggest influence and appreciation is for teachers, in particular, Leigh Reilly, my high school Literature teacher.

Another individual that inspired me greatly was Chisipite Senior School's former Head Girl, Beauty Munodawafa. She was a charismatic, graceful, focused individual that I looked up to and wanted to emulate. Even to this day, if I think of Beauty, I sit up straight!

Was there anyone who noticed your special talent, did you get any moral support?

My teachers, coaches, peers and instructors noticed my talent and the potential that I had—I got moral support from all of these people. However, my biggest form of moral support came from my mother who seldom missed any one of my performances. Knowing that my mother was somewhere in the crowd gave me 'manyemwe' to outshine.

How did people react to you when they noticed you were different—were you understood?

Being the free-spirited person that I am, some of my choices or actions did not come as a surprise. However, I have experienced instances where people, including family, misunderstood my intentions. People with different levels of exposure to artistic backgrounds tend to criticise and misunderstand people that are artistically inclined.

Being Zimbabwean, what were/ are expectations towards you as a female artist/creative being?

I have not been in the "industry" for long; however there are a few misconceptions / prejudices surrounding being a female artist/creative being from Zimbabwe.

What path did you take to follow your vision?

I am still in the process of looking for a mentor. However, social media sites have helped me considerably. By using tools such as Facebook and Twitter, I have managed to, not only interact with a broader audience, but I have been able to share my work with more people than I had ever anticipated.

What is it that you would like to accomplish/ have accomplished (for yourself or anyone) with your creative talent?

I am currently working on my first short story as well as compiling an anthology of some of my poetry. I would like to publish my work and become one of Zimbabwe's leading female authors/poets. Through my social media interactions, I have managed to become an Ambassador for Positive Youth Programs (PYP), a Non—Governmental Organisation that conducts numerous youth based initiatives within Zimbabwe. I am a Columnist for Zimbojam (**www. zimbojam.com**). I would also like to write scripts, act in plays, and be a DJ on radio.

I still have so much that I want to do. However, in everything I do, or have done, I aim to create as many platforms for other talented people as well.

I also recently launched my first solo exhibition in June 2011: ".R.ticulate.R.ebellion", a visual and literal exhibition. Also, earlier this year I was part of a creative experiment titled, ".R.i.O.", which was a fusion of ink and lense (Poetry and Photography).

What do you think could be done to empower creative children (in Zimbabwe)?

There is a colossal need to create more platforms for creative interaction, collaboration and development of creative children in Zimbabwe. An awareness campaign could increase the appreciation of these children's work by society and family. It is extremely difficult to define Zimbabwean culture, so by promoting awareness and inclusion of everyone, this could go a long way in empowering creative children in Zimbabwe.

What message do you have for creative women who feel they have no one to turn to?

Do not let your situation, relationship or background confine or limit your creativity. Work with what you have, learn to be flexible and adapt to the surroundings and environment you are in. Constantly challenge your self to do more, differently, avoid monotony, stagnation and slipping into the comfort zone. Read more, practice longer, engage more, interact with others, network and most importantly, give back. Inspire other women to realise the creativity within them.

http://rutendodenise.blogspot.com

rdmut1@student.monash.edu

Rutendo.denise@yahoo.com

Facebook: http://facebook.com/ RuTendo.DeNise

Twitter: @RutendoDeNise

Twitter: #Knowurzimbos

Cheryl Khumalo "Shishi"

Bio:

SHISHI, born June 10th in Harare, Zimbabwe as Cheryl Khumalo, grew up in a small family and was influenced by music at a young age. She realized the love of music at age thirteen when she joined the high school choir, but Hip Hop was something that she had a passion for. ShiShi began to listen to a lot of female Hip Hop artists like Foxy brown, Lil Kim, Missy Elliot and Da Brat, just to name a few. She studied the way female rappers delivered their music and learned the skill.

In 1997, ShiShi moved to the United States of America to pursue her education, yet her love for Hip Hop continued to grow as she got to understand the Hip Hop culture. While in high school, ShiShi also grew fond of acting and joined the high school theater. ShiShi continued to write her lyrics hoping that one day she would be able to share them with the world, but it wasn't until 2001, after she graduated from Richardson High School, that she decided to take music seriously.

In 2006 ShiShi linked up with Dumisani Maraire Jr and started learning the skills of recording. "Recording didn't come as easily to me as I thought it would but Dumi, Pinnacle and Cee Jay Besa helped me along the way" says ShiShi. Whilst living in Dallas, ShiShi linked up with a Zimbabwean Dancehall artist named Pinnacle and appeared on Pinnacle's Zimotivation mixtape. In 2010, ShiShi became a member of the P.O.A team and was named First Lady of Property of Africa. "I was always at the P.O.A studio and if the Dallas studio was closed, I was at the Rude Boy studio with Cee Jay Besa recording, learning and growing, so I think because I have that hunger as an artist, Dumi (aka Just Lyphe) added me on the P.O.A team and I'm so grateful' she says.

ShiShi is currently working on a mixtape, a debut single, album, her acting career and music videos. ShiShi the Female Rapper is changing the way people look at Hip Hop. "I don't want to be known as another female rapper, I want to be known as the voice that is changing the world through her music. I didn't pick up a mic just to make noise, I picked it up to make a statement."

How were you as a child—was there anything outstanding about your personality?

As a child, I always wanted to be around people. My mother told me that when I was 4 years old, I was playing outside with my friends and noticed other children without toys so I went back into the house, packed all my toys and shared them with everyone on the block. My mom was mad at me because of the fact that she came home and found my room empty of all the toys she had purchased for me, which had been given away; but as time went on, that quality in me helped her and people around me, because it's not always about materialistic value but caring value instead. She told me I always wanted to share and make people happy and I feel that I'm the same way today—I try to reach out to people in my music.

Do you remember when you first realized your talent?

I first realized my talent when I was in high school at the age of 13. I went to an all-girls high school called Harare Roosevelt Girls High. I was a boarder at Delano house; we lived with one of the choir teachers who didn't have enough members in the choir for our school to be entered into a particular competition, so she decided to recruit us for the choir. It was also an advantage for us because we got to travel away from school and our chances of winning were greater because we spent so much time practicing. Practicing was so easy because we lived together. I was happy in Choir and it was then when I realized I had talent in music. I also had the opportunity to study Music at the same time.

Who/what was your inspiration?

My inspiration came from other female artists like Missy Elliot, Eve, Lil Kim, Lauryn Hill, Mary Mary and Whitney Houston, just to name a few. I remember the first album I purchased was Missy Elliot's "Super Dupa Fly" album. When I heard the album, I fell in love with the idea of being a female MC. I listened to and studied the way she delivered her music. The album was so good that I found no reason to skip a track. Hip Hop moved me—the style, the movement, the culture, I was sold and hooked on Hip Hop.

Was there anyone who noticed your special talent, did you get any moral support?

My family has always supported me in my other talents like acting but music was new to them. They knew I was in the choir but never really knew about me as a solo artist. My mother thought I was going to be like my aunt, Musi Khumalo, who was a Radio 3 DJ and ZBC News Anchor. I always looked up to my aunt and wanted to be just like her, but I had to find my own way in the media and I feel that I can do more than rap. I'm working on my acting, writing, producing, and hosting of TV shows. My aunt did push me to go after want I wanted in life and my mother always supported my crazy ideas lol.

How did people react to you when they noticed you were different—were you understood?

I was always different that sometimes I felt misunderstood and kept to myself because I felt alone when I was growing up, but I had a few friends who pushed me and never gave up on me, even when others did. People knew me as the quiet girl in school. Even when my family moved to the United States, I was always the quiet girl because I kept things to myself and was afraid to share who I really was. Once people got to know me, I think their reaction was 'wow you're a cool person to be around'.

Being Zimbabwean, what were/ are expectations towards you as a female artist/creative being?

Being Zimbabwean, my expectations towards me as a female artist are to represent females around the world. Yes I am a Zimbabwean, an African, a woman and a human being. What I am trying to say is, I'm driven by my own expectations due to the fact that I've travelled all around the world and have faced many of my own experiences which characterized my values and expectations.

What path did you take to follow your vision?

I did my own research by reading previous business successes; the paths which others took; listening to information on valuable projects that I found inspiring; asking questions about issues that I felt needed more than just one analysis, because I'm always willing to learn and voice my views. Networking also made it easy for me to share with and learn from other artists. Always remember to do your research!

What is it that you would like to accomplish/ have accomplished (for yourself or anyone) with your creative talent?

I want to accomplish so many things in life—I can't name them all in one day, but I do want to have my own record label one day and be able to support young talented women. Music is always going to be a part of me and I want to get a Grammy one day.

I'm currently writing a script and I'm praying to get to the stages of shooting the film so that I can share it with the world.

What do you think could be done to empower creative children (in Zimbabwe)?

I think what can be done to empower creative children is as simple as taking time for our young children in Zimbabwe and supporting them in what they want to do in life. Once any child knows they have someone who supports their art, it opens so many doors for other things.

What message do you have for creative women who feel they have no one to turn to?

As women we're already strong and we're known for not giving up, so my message for creative women who feel they have no one to turn to is, don't give up, keep knocking on doors and if there is anyone who won't listen to you, *make* them listen. The Internet has also made things easy for anyone, so do your research, learn and be driven

ShiShiMusic@gmail.com

www.facebook.com/shishishe

For bookings: www.poarecords.com

Helen Masvikeni-Masango

Quote:

"The road disappears behind the bend . . . the unknown lies ahead . . . Will it envelope me with joy or will it shower me with tears of pain? However, faith affords me the will to find out." (Helen Masvikeni-Masango)

Bio:

Helen is the definition of an artist! Her work defies categorization and touches areas of the arts such as Dance and Movement; Music; Design and Multimedia; Photography; Literature and Drama. Helen has produced several big dramatic productions that have included all these aspects of the arts to great acclaim. Her group, THE FREEDOM NETWORK, enjoyed great success with their production "FREEDOM", which toured around Zimbabwe performing to sold-out audiences. She continues to work on several artistic productions.

Helen has also taught Dance and Music at Colorado College and at several workshops around the US. She is the owner and Creative Director of Kaffe Emani, a production company which focuses on celebrating art forms such as spoken word, poetry, photography, music, singing, theatre, drama and so much more.

Helen is also an acclaimed photographer . . . . whose work can be viewed under the name, "H. Tafadzwa Photography". For Helen . . . art is life and so . . . to live is art . . . forever.

How were you as a child—was there anything outstanding about your personality?

My personality, both as a child and in adulthood, has been similar . . . with two sides that run parallel. I was an affectionate child who loved to be with people and yet had such introverted tendencies, which would find me stealing away for many private moments where I enjoyed being in my mind. I am the same way as an adult.

Do you remember when you first realized your talent?

I think because I am into many forms of art, the realization happened in different eras of my life. I realized that at the very early age of five that I loved dance and it wasn't until I was an adult, that I realised my deep desire for Photography. I am still evolving and making discoveries.

Who/what was your inspiration?

My inspirations didn't have anything to do with my art forms. My mother and sister inspired me at an early age. My sister inspired me to be the best and to reach for the top because she is that way and my mother inspired me to be a person who strives for depth in the midst of hardship. She is a clear example of the true definition of meekness. She is strength under control.

The inspiration of the art in me is God. He birthed it in me, nurtured it and continues to amaze me in all that He has done and continues to do. That alone inspires me!

Was there anyone who noticed your special talent, did you get any moral support?

I have had several people along the way who noticed the talent in me. I had a dance instructor called Clayton Ndlovu who pulled out the dancer in me. I attribute my dance desire and ability to him. At another stage in my life, my Pastor, Noah Pashapa, looked past the dreadlocked girl who was misunderstood and saw a girl with a great desire to worship the Lord using these art forms. He gave me a chance in the church to do this, even when others told him not to. Looking back, I see that if it had not been for him, I would not be me . . . now.

How did people react to you when they noticed you were different—were you understood?

For the most part, I was misunderstood. The things I did were dubbed as 'only Helen could do that' things. I wasn't understood, but for the most part I was accepted and embraced. The relational part of me got me accepted and by the time they tried to back out of the art in me . . . it was too late. Lol!

Being Zimbabwean, what were/are expectations towards you as a female artist/creative being?

Being Zimbabwean, being a woman, being black . . . all these things drew different expectations from different groups of people. It is too much to expound on, however. It presented different fights to win and different bridges to cross that either knocked me down at first or backed me up against a wall, but I conquered them all. To this day, these three factors still present fights and bridges, but I welcome them and overcome.

What path did you take to follow your vision?

I've been at this for a while. There are things that I do now that I would have done way earlier had I known to do them. To summarize all my lessons learnt, I believe one should find a person, organization etc that is doing it well and learn . . . learn . . . learn! If you want to be excellent at something, going at it alone might get you there, but it will take longer. To emulate is not a bad thing . . . just don't lose yourself. Work hard . . . but don't forget to work smart, too. And then lastly . . . give it your all as you have fun with it. What good is it to achieve something you love but hate the process? Give it your all so that you don't have any regrets. It's worth it!!

What is it that you would like to accomplish/ have accomplished (for yourself or anyone) with your creative talent?

I want to accomplish many things . . . but mostly success and satisfaction. I want to be able to stand before God one day and have Him say, "well done! You did well with what I gave you and you did me proud". I don't want to squander time, talent and opportunity. I want to be a success with it also. Whether it is monetary or otherwise . . . I want it. I believe that because we are humans, this means something to us and I also believe that your gift must make room for you.

What do you think could be done to empower creative children (in Zimbabwe)?

A school of arts! This is my hope, my plan for Zimbabwe.

What message do you have for creative women who feel they have no one to turn to?

As long as it is what God has said for you to do, He will make it happen for you. I think that a healthy, tenacious grip on whatever that art form may be is necessary. Also know that others before you have done it and so can you. When you can wrap your mind around truths like this . . . the rest is up to you. Learn, do . . . do it well and you will not go wrong. Opportunity will come and you better be found ready!

www.zviwanegallery.com

www.facebook.com—H. Tafadzwa Photography

Charlene Kunira

Quote of your choice:

"In life there is a time for everything." (Author unknown)

Bio:

Charlene Kunira was born in Harare, Zimbabwe and left for the UK at the age of 17 to pursue her studies at Middlesex University. She completed her degree in Project Management at Middlesex University in 2006.

Charlene has worked in London's Premiere Photographic/Model Portfolio studios in the West End, London in the Advertising and Model Business Contracts sector. After over five years experience in the industry, Charlene continued to pursue her studies and is now an Affiliate Member of the Chartered Management Institute, United Kingdom.

She is currently the Co-Founder and Host for the ever so popular Zimchictv.com (www.zimchictv.com). This is a brand new video blog featuring show biz updates and a social network providing a platform for the urban artists Zimchictv promotes. It also showcases and empowers artists from all urban backgrounds, who are making huge achievements in their careers.

How were you as a child—was there anything outstanding about your personality?

I have always been a happy, cheerful person and I grew up with no brothers and sisters until the age of 16. I was always very sociable and was able to find creative ways to entertain myself when I was at home, including always having friends over for sleep-over parties.

Do you remember when you first realized your talent?

I realised that I had talent when I presented a poem and acted in school dramas confidently. Over the years people would comment positively on my performances.

Who/what was your inspiration?

My mother is my inspiration because she has always supported me even when I would get my ideas and presentations wrong. She has always encouraged me to follow my dreams

Was there anyone who noticed your special talent, did you get any moral support?

I have had immense support from work colleagues, family, church members and members of Human Rights organisations. I have campaigned for several Human Rights Organisations against the violation of women's rights.

How did people react to you when they noticed you were different—were you understood?

I have never really been misunderstood; people have always respected and understood me for the most part.

Being Zimbabwean, what were/ are expectations towards you as a female artist/creative being?

As a Zimbabwean, I am expected to make the content of my creativity suitable with respect to the audience, not only to Zimbabweans, but also to other nationalities.

What path did you take to follow your vision?

More recently, I now have a Manager who mentors me and gives advice on different contracts and am starting workshops on Acting /Presenting /Public speaking. ZimchicTV has a website; a page on Facebook which we use for marketing and we make use of other social networks. When we first started, sending out hundreds of emails until we got any answers was difficult, as the audience was skeptical and wanted to see more before they signed up on the website. However, as they grew to know us, it got easier.

What is it that you would like to accomplish/ have accomplished (for yourself or anyone) with your creative talent?

We hope to continue to encourage artists to be more confident with their music presentation, styling and provide a platform of a high standard for artists to advertise their work professionally.

What do you think could be done to empower creative children (in Zimbabwe)?

When you are a creative child, presentation and confidence are attributes that need to be continuously nurtured and respected in order to get an audience and support. This will help them to be able to tackle any challenge that comes across their path as they grow.

What message do you have for creative women who feel they have no one to turn to?

Always research the sector that you have an interest in, so as to keep updated. Do not be disheartened by negative feedback and never give up.

—

Please Subscribe and keep watching:
www.zimchictv.com

Maureen Chengetayi Chidavaenzi

Quote of your choice:

"Today is a blessing, Another Day and Another Opportunity. Be A Winner not a Whiner. WINNERS make things happen and WHINERS make excuses. Look in the mirror and see if you are a WINNER or a WHINER."

Bio:

Maureen Chengetayi Chidavaenzi is a native of the motherland Southern Africa (Malawi and Zimbabwe), born 11 July in 1967. She is the Senior Staff Assistant at the Southeast Center for Photographic Studies Department at Daytona State College. She has been with the college for more than a few years and is very well known for her optimistic and positive character.

Originally from Zimbabwe, Maureen is a well-travelled social entrepreneur who enjoys meeting people from diverse backgrounds. She has a passion for Health & Wellness and owns a few turn-key businesses that promote Health and Wellness. In addition, Maureen holds a Bachelors degree in Supervision and Management and is a former employee of Bethune Cookman University, where she worked for 12 years in several departments.

Additionally, she has worked for the Daytona Beach Police Department, non-profits and Fortune 500 corporate organizations.

She is exceedingly active in her community; she spends countless hours volunteering in many civic duties such as serving as an active member of the Citizen Observation Police Patrol; she is a Drug and Rehabilitation Counsellor and a certified Sunday School Teacher at the local Salvation Army. She has received many awards from the community including the 2010 Best Citizen Volunteer Award from the Chief of Police, Michael Chitwood. She sits on several boards in the Volusia County area.

Maureen also holds a Diploma in Modeling, Film and Acting from Silhouettes Studios in Harare, Zimbabwe. She has modelled and participated in fashion shows both in Zimbabwe and Florida USA. In her spare time, she enjoys spending time with her family and friends, as well as singing throughout the state with her travelling Caribbean band.

Maureen is the manager for her two boys, A2Z: Recording Artists-Writer-Actors-Models. Maureen says music is her passion and therapy. Maureen describes herself to be a motivator, ambitious, understanding, righteous, entrepreneurial, eloquent, noble, confident, hospitable, energetic, nourishing, generous, ethical, thankful, appreciative, youthful and independent.

How were you as a child—was there anything outstanding about your personality?

Ever since childhood, I was very mature and advanced in many ways compared to other children of the same age. I was very creative, honest and hardworking. I always strived to do everything by myself to please my parents. I never wanted to do anything that would disappoint them or anyone else because they thought so highly of me. My late father always referred to me as "his mother" and I never understood what he meant until I grew up to be a young adult. I asked him why he called me his mother and he told me that I'd always had so much wisdom for my age ever since I could talk and he was so proud of me, which made him respect me as much as his own mother. I was always nurturing and caring towards my siblings, family, friends and everyone around me. I always led and I can recall my parents telling me that I would be a leader one day, which always stuck in my head.

Do you remember when you first realized your talent?

I recognized that I was talented when I got to primary school, perhaps in the 5th grade, when my teacher mentioned it to me. I was not sure what my specific talent was because I was interested in various things such as sewing, cooking, singing, dancing, decorating, modelling, acting, drawing, basketball, track and event planning. At that time I was just doing and joining a lot of activities until I got to high school and started realizing what I really enjoyed the most. At the end of high school I realized I was more of an artist . . . I really never parted with anything to do with music, modelling and acting.

Who/what was your inspiration?

My mother (my angel), both my grandfathers and grandmothers (entrepreneurs and hard workers), my first cousins, Rosemary Kumitsonyo-Kanyuka, Nelson Mandela, The late First Lady Sally Mugabe, Mama Africa Miriam Makeba, Princess Diana Spencer, Paul Simon, Diana Ross, Donna Summer, Lionel Richie, George Benson, Yvonne Chaka Chaka, Brenda Fasi, Bob Marley and The I Threes (Yvonne Judy Mowatt, Marcia Griffiths, Rita Marley). I was inspired by their integrity, diligence, humility and powerful qualities.

Was there anyone who noticed your special talent, did you get any moral support?

My grandmother (from my mother's side), who lives in Malawi, used to tell my mom that I was a very special and talented child. I had an American basketball coach who also told me that I was talented. I never took it seriously until I came to the United States where many people noticed my talents, showered me with compliments and pushed me into singing and doing many other community activities. I feel as though I never got any moral support from Zimbabwe. This may be because of our culture in which it is rare for people to notice talents such as singing, acting, etc. It is viewed as being different, naughty, abnormal or disobedient. Therefore, I was pushed into academics and discouraged to pursue my passion as an artist. I really wanted to sing, model and act, but I was told that it was not a career and that instead I should go to school and get a degree which would lead me to be a lawyer, doctor, executive and all the other white collar positions.

How did people react to you when they noticed you were different—were you understood?

Many people didn't understand me at all; many thought I was unusual, overconfident, and mischievous. At first it bothered me, but I got to the point where I had to pursue what made me content. As long as I convinced my parents to trust me and let me do what I really wanted to do, I stopped pleasing people and got blessings from my parents.

Thank God that they understood me, gave me their blessings to go to a modelling school and come to the USA to chase my talents.

It really took me being in the USA, to find my real talents on my own because I was hungry to be an artist. Fortunately, when my parents found out I was singing they said they were okay with it and told me that as long as I am happy with what I want to do, they would give me their blessings.

Being Zimbabwean, what were/are expectations towards you as a female artist/creative being?

It is really difficult for me to tell because I actually didn't pursue much of my career in Zimbabwe as it was not accepted as a successful career and looked at as something not lady-like. I had no one that guided me into what I really wanted to do, so I ended up doing things to please my family and was afraid to disappoint or embarrass them. The only thing I initiated on my own in Zimbabwe was attending the modelling school, which I did a little before I came to the USA.

What path did you take to follow your vision?

I started on my career path after I met a good friend of mine, Drewe, who was managing a lot of Caribbean bands. He thought

I was extremely talented, creative and that I had a beautiful voice and personality. I never took him seriously until he started taking me to different gigs with bands. One day he told the band to call me up on stage to do a cover song that I used to sing in the car when I was with him. The first time I did the cover song by Yellow man, the band asked me if I could work with them. I was amazed because I never thought I was that good since I had only sung for fun before.

Drewe convinced me he was going to be my manager and was going to start getting me gigs with different Caribbean bands. He became my mentor and manager. I never took lessons; it just came naturally to me. I started freelancing and performing with various bands whenever they needed a female artist. So the bottom line is that it started as a hobby, having fun with karaoke and just jumping on the stage here and there to do one or two songs with different bands and reggae artists, until my stage name was well known—"Sistah Maureen the Empress". After that, Drewe had so many calls coming in to book me and I even had to turn down some gigs because I couldn't keep up with so many of them, I can only do so much.

What is it that you would like to accomplish/ have accomplished (for yourself or anyone) with your creative talent?

Right now I am managing my two boys A2Z, mentoring them and working so hard towards my goal for them to be signed by a big major record label. I told them that I wish I had the support I give them compared to my parents who are from the old who highly supported me academically, but not my talent to be a recording artist. For that reason, I would like to ensure A2Z make it really BIG to fulfill my dream as a recording artist. Their accomplishment will make me so happy because regardless of how passionate I am about my music and am enjoying every moment of it, it is not an easy task. I am determined that A2Z will make it soon with the support and guidance I am giving them as their mother and Managing Director.

What do you think could be done to empower creative children (in Zimbabwe)?

To be the best role model by supporting each other and particularly our new generation. To empower them and build their self esteem by allowing them to follow their talents.

What message do you have for creative women who feel they have no one to turn to?

Keep on keeping—pushing and fighting to achieve your passion and dream. The sky is the limit, anyone can make it if they try and never get discouraged. Do not allow anyone to tell you that you cannot do this and that. You are what you speak, think, or want. If you want the best to come to you, you must speak the best of you, strive for the best, work hard and you will get there. All the best to everyone that wants to follow their DREAM.

Extra info

Who is A2Z? If you haven't heard of A2Z; PLEASE Check Them Out By Simply Visiting http://www.facebook.com/pages/A2Z/137879809586069 or www.a2zswag.com/

Share the gifts of peace, kindness, and heartfelt generosity each day! The first Wealth is definitely your HEALTH Check Out your OPTIMAL HEALTH products ON THE WEB!!!for Health/Fitness/Beauty & Gifts Of Choice @ www.ChroniclesGlobal.com

Gloria Rumbidzai Ndoro-Mkombachoto

Quote of your choice:

"There can be only one success, one accomplishment, one fulfillment and one source of peace, joy and happiness—and that is to spend your life, your very own CHOSEN way, regardless of what others think of it. If you aren't living life your CHOSEN way right now, then it might just turn out to be a wasted & failed life." (Gloria Rumbidzai Ndoro-Mkombachoto)

Bio:

Gloria Ndoro is the Chief Executive Officer and Managing Consultant of Global Business Assignments Incorporated, a Management Consulting firm she started in 1991 with a single focus: to assist CEOs and their top management teams develop their organizations in order that they effectively deliver their business and organizational strategies.

Previously, Gloria lectured in Financial and Management Accounting for Business and International Marketing to undergraduates and MBA students respectively at the University of Zimbabwe; Finance and Management to Honours students and Post-Graduate Students respectively at the University of Cape Town; Strategy and Entrepreneurship to MBA, Management Advancement Programme and Masters In Management to students at the University of Witwatersrand; Graduate School of Business (WBS) and in the Management and Executive Development Programmes of both WBS and University of Stellenbosch, Graduate School of Business.

Gloria has been consulting since 1988 when she came back to Africa from Canada where she had graduated in the MBA Programme at the University of Ottawa. The MBA was embarked on after finishing a Bachelor of Commerce Degree at the University of Swaziland in 1984. Gloria is currently completing her Doctorate in Informatics and Design at the Cape Peninsula University of Technology.

She has consulted widely for the private sector, public sector and the international community, such as IFC/WORLD BANK, AMSCO, USAID, UNDP, UNIFEM, UNIDO, NORAD, Royal Danish Embassy, ESAMI in Southern and Eastern Africa and Afghanistan. In the private & public sectors, she has consulted, created & reviewed strategies for several organizations including but not restricted to the following: Seed Co, the African Seed Company, Standard Bank of SA, Zimbabwe Open University, Omega Transport and Security, Delta Corporation, Global Foreign Exchange, SA National Productivity Institute etc.

Gloria is also a Decorative Artist and is the sole design capability behind all the wrought iron creations (ornamental furniture, decorative artworks and collectibles) at Totem Shumba Metal Studio @ Totem Shumba Estate, a business she started in 2009. The business started off as a hobby where she wanted to explore her creative abilities and is fast growing into a business with export markets. Gloria also has business interests in the property and food sectors in Southern Africa. She lives in both Zimbabwe and South Africa, the region where her business interests are concentrated.

How were you as a child—was there anything outstanding about your personality?

Determined and undeterred—are the two words that sum up who I was growing up. I grew up with a sense of focus and with an attitude that nothing was insurmountable if you put your mind to it. To a certain extent, that made me become a control freak. If I wanted something badly, I got it. Failure was never an option for me. I have recently started realizing that it is okay to let go and it is a complete and well-lived life if you do not get to have everything you want. Happiness, peace, tranquility, good health and most importantly, doing what you want when you want to, have become cherished priorities.

Do you remember when you first realized your talent?

When did I first realize my talent you ask? Which particular talent? I consider myself multi-talented. If academics is an art form, I realized at junior school that participating in class allowed me to internalize concepts. In high school I realized that I needed to study in order to score exceptional grades and at University, I realized that I had to attend all lectures in order to sail through because it was in class that the lecturer emphasized sections that one should know in order to pass that subject.

The art arena was somewhat tricky for me. I realized in high school that I was artistically inclined but never uttered a word to my parents because art was not encouraged in my family. My father always announced to us that most artists were poor people and he was never going to allow any of his children to choose a poor life for as long as he was alive. A young brother of mine, the fourth in the family, lived, dreamt, and did art day in and day out. He suffered the brunt of the criticism from my father and as a result became reclusive in his room. He would lock himself up and not speak to anyone whilst sketching artworks in his room. When I saw this, I decided that I would never ever confide in anyone that in fact I had desires of my own that I wanted to pursue. I therefore became the exemplary first born, good girl and settled for academics. I decided at a young age that if most artists were indeed poor, I would first succeed at academics and then, with a bag of cash in hand, I would then have the latitude and "luxury" to pursue my area of art.

Who/what was your inspiration?

My mother was an artistic person in the way she cooked, laid out her food, decorated her home, the antique pieces she bought and the way she arranged them in the house. Not only that, for a woman who was a qualified nursing sister, she did amazing embroidery (cross stitch mainly), crocheted and knitted all our winter jerseys for many years and sold many more, in addition to sewing most of our clothes. At one time she was working full-time and supplying Barbours with her sewn wares. Although now a retired nurse, she is still a fantastic cook, still knits, sews and crochets. I was very keen and excelled in hardanger embroidery at high school.

Was there anyone who noticed your special talent, did you get any moral support?

My mother and Domestic Science teacher noticed my artistic talents and nurtured them.

How did people react to you when they noticed you were different—were you understood?

I grew up in a family where we were told everyday that the sky was the limit. Yet, outside the security and confines of that family was the real world that filtered what a girl child could and could not do. I realized when I was at high school that there were different expectations by the society from a girl child which were different from that of a boy child. To a large extent, I believe I was traumatized somewhat, but I carried on to this day. Not being understood has never bothered me. I am not a needy person, who thrives on acceptance and validation from other people because I believe alone, I am complete.

Being Zimbabwean, what were/ are expectations towards you as a female artist/creative being?

Depending on the art discipline you excel in, the expectations and perceptions vary somewhat but generally speaking, within the black community, artists are not well regarded. Most are perceived to be losers, out of touch with reality, who will live a life of scrounging and die as losers. That is why parents do not ordinarily support children who want to pursue a career in the arts. The argument which is not tired and sounds like a stuck record is that, it is a career that leads one way, down the path to poverty because not many people support the arts. I believe the white community and younger and progressive black parents are much more encouraging to their kids to pursue the arts.

I became an artist via the back door, by studying what brings food and fortune on the table first and then getting back to it at a later day after having achieved self actualization. It is a long and sometimes frustrating journey, but I believe it is a journey that has paid off because, right now, I am not producing my creations for cash, but for the love of it. After I design a product and we have created it in my workshop, if it does not appeal to me to be good enough to be in my home, office or my outdoors, I rework it. My attitude is that if it is not good enough for me, it cannot be good enough for my customers.

I believe I am lucky because the target market for my wrought iron creations are people who I perceive to be like me and are classified for marketing purposes to be within the same living standards measure (LSM). It is working and myself and my team love what we are doing because we have a long term view on this, money has ceased to be a priority. When you stop pursuing money and you create for the sheer love of your creativity, the integrity and honesty in your work shows and the money will start pursuing you.

What path did you take to follow your vision?

I have already mentioned before that although I was a creative person, I "parked it" for years whilst I studied Business Management at undergraduate and graduate levels. That helped a lot because in my past career which I have retired from, I was a private sector Development Consultant and one of the areas I focused on, was how to get people to be sustainable entrepreneurs. Business as a discipline comes naturally because my parents, although they were professionals, were enterprising. Later my father set up a chain of businesses. I believe that when you have family and friends in business it rubs off. What also helps is to surround yourself with people who are business-minded.

I market on Facebook, in Magazines that target the same LSM market as ourselves. Advertisements are expensive, but as we are building the brand, we are pouring everything into the enterprise. I see my creativity in wrought iron products for indoor and outdoor as a business, not a small project that is done half-heartedly. My background in private sector development has allowed me to be bullish in how we engage and get people to know about our business.

Most importantly, we (myself and my staff) worship the ground on which our customers walk, literally, because we know, without customers, we go hungry. I believe we do a great job at it, because although we have got a clear cut marketing strategy, most of our sales are from word of mouth. We ask new customers how they got to know of us and most tell us that they were recommended to us by an existing customer, visitor and so on. Right now, very few people have come to us through advertising in targeted media. Perhaps our investment in advertising will pay off in the future, but right now we do not have any empirical data on the ground to prove that advertising is producing desired sales.

What is it that you would like to accomplish/ have accomplished (for yourself or anyone) with your creative talent?

My creative talent is allowing me to consolidate my financial freedom whilst ensuring that I remain in a happy, peaceful, tranquil, free emotional and physical space. I am able to assist the less privileged, through my Foundation—the Shumba Huru Foundation. My creative talent is allowing me to live my best life whilst creating employment for many; at the same time I get to meet many other creative people, share and benefit from the cross—pollination of ideas.

What do you think could be done to empower creative children (in Zimbabwe)?

In order to empower creative children in Zimbabwe, two things stand out as follows:

1. Creativity must be part and parcel of the school curriculum. This will help in encouraging creative children to excel earlier on in their lives. One of the major differences between public and private schools in Zimbabwe is that private schools consciously set aside creative spaces for children and public schools do not.
2. We need to have accredited small niche colleges or institutes focusing on the Creative Arts, run by successful creative people.

What message do you have for creative women who feel they have no one to turn to?

My message to creative women is that you have got to be willing to make sacrifices, great sacrifices. Most importantly, you have to fear poverty and make poverty your enemy. When you settle for less, most times you end up getting far much more less than the less you had bargained for. Creative women ought to realize that in life you do not necessarily get what you deserve, but what you negotiate.

The challenges facing creative women are not unique to them alone. Many other women embarking on creative careers face similar challenges associated with lack of familial support, not having a support group that motivates and encourages you, access to financing, markets and so on.

It however becomes more challenging for creative women who focus on a predominantly "inspired creative career path". By "inspired creative career path", I mean those who are willing to produce only the stuff that is inspired from their dreams, journeys, experiences, etc and whose production of these artworks is not necessarily aligned to market needs. When your creativity is not what the market demands, it means the market is not going to pay for whatever it is you are creating and therefore you can easily go hungry. When you are a creative woman, who is operating in an environment of inadequate resources, it tampers with your creativity because you are now spending your time worrying about bread and butter issues. When you are worried about food, shelter, clothing, transport and fees—basic needs according to the Maslow's hierarchy of needs, it becomes very difficult for you to achieve self actualization in your creativity.

I am now very thankful to my late father for literally frog-marching me towards academics. Having post graduate qualifications and working in academia and private sector Development Consulting for more than twenty years has allowed me to achieve financial security which has provided the softer landing that has enabled me to launch my creative career. I started concentrating on my creative abilities in my mid-forties, a late starter at that because I had mastered this lesson: that when you are hungry and worried about the provision of basic needs, it tampers with your creative abilities. I did not want to end up poor and at the same time failing to explore my creative abilities to my maximum potential. As a result, I started elsewhere where I was still creative but not producing visible products like I am now.

I lectured in Strategy, Marketing and Entrepreneurship and consulted in the same areas in private sector Development Consulting. You need to be creative in order to be a great organizational strategist, marketer and entrepreneur! It is the same creative mind that is allowing me to pursue my current creative career.

In terms of making great sacrifices, I left my creature comforts in Zimbabwe and lived in many countries in sub-Saharan Africa and South East Asia. My children paid the ultimate price of being in boarding schools and not being with their mother during some holidays. During these periods, I saved money and changed my diet eating only one-minute noodles and tinned sardines. I never however cut back on my dry red wine, gin and tonic and whisky!

Every creative woman's journey will be different and peppered with many interesting and challenging stories; however key traits such as perseverance, determination, commitment, sacrifice, tenacity and razor sharp focus will be common to most women's journeys. Whatever journey you take, direct or indirect, pot-holed or not, I suggest that you have fun and a great sense of humour whilst doing it.

Email : gloria.ndoro@yahoo.com

Blog: www.gloriandorounfiltered. blogspot.com

Interview with Michelle Ashburner : **http://www.southafricansyoushouldmeet. com/**

(Websites under construction): www.totemshumba.com www.gloriandoro.com www.gbaincorporated.biz

Quote:

"I flow from my heart so I can touch your heart . . ." (Yiangshi—inspired by her younger brother, the late Tafadzwa 'Uz' Uzande).

Bio:

Yiangshi aka Yvonne Vimbainashe Uzande is a Zimbabwean Singer /Songwriter/ Producer/Artist currently based in Canada. Under her production company, Yeshua & Yiangshi, she has produced Zimbabwe national radio hits such as "Semvura", "Amai" (acoustic guitar version), "Mavambo" co-produced with Sody aka Tafadzwa Soda and Nyasha Makambira and "Munoziva" co-produced with Sody.

Her debut album, "Zvemwoyo: Love Story", produced by Cee Jay of Rude-Boy Records which was released in Dallas, USA 2003, was a major success along with "Semvura", which was featured on Sanii Makhalima's compilation album, "Walala Wasala" along with other hit tunes such as "Thrill aka Budweiser" and "Amai".

Yiangshi proceeded to record an acoustic project, "Face to Face" in 2004 and "Sozo" (Greek for salvation) in 2008, dedicated to her late younger brother, Uz aka Tafadzwa Uzande.

Currently she is working on a new bombshell of a project titled, "Holding Hands", due to be released in 2011-2012, produced primarily by Nyasha Makambira. This fresh side of Yiangshi highlights her growth as a musician and the depth of her heart as she expresses issues close to her heart in creative musical vibes. This album features themes ranging from love, friendship, enemies, broken relationships, intimacy with God, faith, family, evangelism and thankfulness. She is featuring popular fellow musicians such as Jus Lyphe aka Dumi Maraire and Wizzy Mangoma based in the USA; Yardsteppa based in Canada; May J based in Australia; MC Mighty in Ireland; DJ Gabz TC ONE, Terry '1Kg' Jay, and Dancehall Ambassador Jusa in the UK; Zviwane in the USA and JD aka Janelle Deegan based in Canada, to mention a few. The music genres in this eclectic-reflective project range from rave, acoustic, ragga, dancehall, rhumba, afro-jazz, pop, rnb, to reggae. Her desire is for people to hear God's voice behind her voice, to reflect deeply upon the lyrics of her songs and to glean solid truth from her messages.

Apart from music, Yiangshi has also produced various fine art pieces majoring in Figure Drawing, Still Life paintings and Imaginative Compositions. She has exhibited her artwork at various art shows and art galleries in Harare, Zimbabwe. She has also written a poetic compilation of poetry for Zimbabwe, which aims to highlight her emotions towards her native country's current socio-political and economic situation, as well as her hope for its restoration.

After her student exchange year in Belgium, when she was still a teen, she developed a love for languages and often uses her knowledge of French, English, Shona and Spanish in her creative expressions. She believes that learning other languages bridges the gap in the cultural divide.

Yiangshi has also participated in Drama, taking part in various plays and winning awards for Best Actress during her high school years. She took part in English and French Public Speaking as well as debates, so she has deeply immersed herself in the creative arts on various dimensions.

In all her creative endeavors, be they music compositions, song-writing, poetry, painting, drawing, acting, delivery of speeches or debating, Yiangshi's principal desire is for her creativity to inspire positive change in people's lives—she flows from the heart so that she can touch the heart of others. That is her legacy . . .

How were you as a child—was there anything outstanding about your personality?

As a child, I was very inquisitive and eager to explore new things. I was very intellectual, loved reading books, listening to music, drawing, painting, writing poetry and eventually learned to play the guitar, after which I started composing my own songs at the age of 12. I think one thing that stood out about my personality was my desire to learn and be knowledgeable in as many areas as possible As a result, I developed a very creative and inspired mind and this led me to pursue creativity from then until now.

Do you remember when you first realized your talent?

I think I always thought talent was natural, so to me I didn't really have a specific point when I realized that I was talented in the arts. Being artistic and creative was just an inborn quality, a part of my personality that was planted in me by my Creator even before I was born. So I was always aware of my creative instinct from a very young age and as I grew up and tapped more into this instinct, my realization of my creative gift strengthened and grew as I took steps to develop these inborn divine talents.

Who/what was your inspiration?

Various elements have influenced my creative journey as I have finally defined myself creatively.

My most significant influence is God-Creator. I think He is the most creative and inspiring being I have EVER encountered. He breathes ideas and thoughts into my spirit as I pour out to Him about my life, my goals and supernaturally songs start flowing, tunes begin forming, creativity is stimulated, words arise and I just cannot explain how marvelous the creative process is when its source is from the source of all Art and Creation: GOD HIMSELF! My Christian faith definitely inspires me the most in my creative expressions.

My mother Cecilia 'The Queen' Uzande has been another source of inspiration for me. A strong, confident and gifted woman, she taught me all I know about expressing myself in words and song as she herself is talented in those fields. She imparted all her knowledge to me and for that I am ever-grateful.

Another inspiration is my late brother, Tafadzwa 'UZ' Uzande, a Rhema Bible College pastor who was tragically killed in a car accident in South Africa in 2004. He was an amazing Hip Hop artist performing all over Africa with his Congolese friend, Andre Katombe. Uz taught me that in order to touch people I had to simplify my message for all to understand and I always had to deliver my gift to the world from the depth of a sincere heart. I thank him for his wisdom. May he rest in peace.

I would also say that I find inspiration from my other family members, who in their own ways, impart knowledge and wisdom to me that helps me express myself the way I do. My Dad, who is a source of great English vocabulary as he was once a Headmaster and English teacher,

is also uplifting and humorous. Millies, my elder sister, has taught me eloquence and faith in myself and my gifts. Emmah, my other sister, is a great exhorter. Petra, another sister, is a musical inspiration with a great voice and with amazing songwriting skills: she is my fierce critical creative advisor and supporter. Eddie, my older brother, is my number one fan who sings ALL my songs and always knows the right thing to say to inspire me, especially on a bad day or when I lack inspiration: he is amazing!

And finally my current music producers, Nyasha Makambira and Corey Bitner have also deeply inspired my talents—always urging me to strive for a higher level of excellence, creating just the right musical vibes and effects to enhance the impact of my music. These guys have encouraged me to grow from strength to strength as an artist. I cherish them: they are God-given.

Was there anyone who noticed your special talent, did you get any moral support?

My family noticed my talent and urged me to pursue my gift in the Creative Arts, especially my mother who would teach me all she knew about music and song. My Headmistress, Sister Gundula, also saw the potential in me and encouraged my participation in creative activities throughout my high school years at the Dominican Convent, Harare. My producers Cee Jay Besa and Nyasha Makambira saw my potential and made it possible for me to begin recording my work and start my career. Sanii and Delani Makalima, fellow musicians, also recognized my talent and featured me on a musical compilation, which opened doors for my music to be played on Zimbabwe national radio.

How did people react to you when they noticed you were different—were you understood?

I am so glad that people embraced and celebrated my uniqueness. I tried to keep my creative expressions simple but at the same time, deep and meaningful. I think people appreciate it when an individual dares to express themselves in an original, but easy to understand manner. I like to think that I was understood and I felt that my creativity was well received.

Being Zimbabwean, what were/ are expectations towards you as a female artist/creative being?

Being an artist, whether male or female, has always been a challenge in Zimbabwe especially since art is often viewed as of lesser importance compared to the sciences or more technical gifting. I'm not sure I was or am aware of what people's

expectations are towards me as a female Zimbabwean artist, but I do know that I have to work harder to be heard, appreciated and acknowledged for my creative expressions—I have to be really excellent in my arts so as to be recognized as being part of the highest caliber of artists. It is challenging but enjoyable all the same.

What path did you take to follow your vision?

There were seven specific steps I took in following my vision:

1. I committed my vision to my Creator
   I have a deep God-faith and in all I do, I put Him first. I prayed over my vision for divine favor and empowerment to accomplish the vision.
2. I searched my bible for inspiring scriptures that would encourage me along the way, especially the book of Psalms and Songs of Solomon, which are the most beautiful poetic and melodic books in the Bible for me.
3. I wrote down what I wanted to accomplish so the vision was clear in my head: I wrote my desires to one day record the songs I had

written, themes I wanted to write about, the audience I wanted to reach and ways I would try to reach them. I regularly visited my list of goals to gauge my progress.

4. I began investing in and watering my talent i.e. composing songs regularly, writing poetry, involving myself in creative activities such as art lessons at the gallery, joining the choir, forming a guitar club, participating in public speaking and debating competitions, learning languages, joining the drama group and REPTeens, participating in musical evenings and concerts, forming a singing group etc.

5. I searched for mentors in the fields I am interested in, there is great wisdom in those that have already achieved what you are striving to also achieve. I began to learn how to go about recording my music, writing songs, etc.

6. I searched for a network of creative people who could contribute to my arts, enhance my creativity, add to my expression and as I opened myself up more to other artists, I grew and expanded my audience as I collaborated with other artists. Networks such as Myspace, Soundclick and Facebook were amongst some of the most helpful tools in making creative connections as well as getting linked with artists in my surrounding community such as church, work etc.

7. I found ways, even grassroots level ways, of marketing myself and continued to research new ways to make myself and my arts known to the world i.e. by featuring on collaborations; I coordinated creative arts workshops at local libraries; shared my music with friends and encouraged them to share with their friends etc; created profiles on Myspace, Soundclick, Facebook; I sold my CD's wherever possible at church, work, school, in Zimbabwe and nowadays it is easy to market one's work on Amazon, Cdbaby and Itunes to mention a few. I took part in various concerts, sent my music to various DJs and they played them not only on Internet radio stations, but also on national radio in my home country.

What is it that you would like to accomplish/ have accomplished (for yourself or anyone) with your creative talent?

My primary purpose in life is to spread the Truths expressed in the message of Christ's love for all of us, how He came and taught us about excellent living and enjoying our lives as we make the most of the gifts that God gave us: this is my goal as I pursue my creative exploits. I love to express important messages about God, about life and how to overcome its challenges by faith, hope and positive thinking.

I look forward to continuing to record my songs, write and perform all over the world. I desire to leave a heart legacy . . . that people will remember me for touching their hearts through my creative productions—for bringing light and revelation to the confused; joy and upliftment to the depressed; love and laughter to the unwanted; truth and wisdom to the searching. I find great joy when fans give me feedback that my song has touched their lives in a special way—that is a reward all in itself.

What do you think could be done to empower creative children (in Zimbabwe)?

There are three important things that I think can be done to empower creative children in Zimbabwe:

1. Invest financially into the development of creative programs and workshops for children in Zimbabwe. In particular, for those in the diaspora, any funds we can spare to help those in less fortunate countries are appreciated!

2. Create platforms for children to express themselves e.g. poetry competitions, singing and dance extravaganzas, music soirees, open mic events—if those of us who can find sponsors for those types of events can get companies or organizations interested, this will be an amazing idea.

3. Personally invest in the children's lives by continuing to impart creativity through sharing our creative works with our homeland and not just spreading our work in the Diaspora: reaching out to the children to show them what we have so they too can learn from us.

What message do you have for creative women who feel they have no one to turn to?

I would like to encourage the creative woman who feels that she has no one to turn to by saying, keep creating and cultivating your gift. Plant it wherever you go, water it with your active works, share it with everyone you meet. Open your heart to the wisdom of other artists and learn from them. Do not doubt your ability or look down upon yourself—even when it seems no one understands your vision, press on and one day your breakthrough will dawn like a beautiful sunrise. Have faith in your creativity and even if you start at grassroots level to make yourself seen, heard and appreciated, cherish the smaller steps, which lead to larger leaps, which lead to an open world of your success.

Thanks & Acknowledgements

I would like to thank God, my family and fans for all their support and encouragement: you make all my creative efforts worthwhile.

www.myspace.com/yyjvz

Facebook : "Yiangshi Uzzy"

Facebook Band Page: "Yeshua & Yiangshi"

Soundclick username: Yiangshi

Email: yiangshiuzzy@gmail.com *or* **yiangshimusik@hotmail.com**

Music Sampling: www.youtube. com, search for and subscribe to "YIANGSHI"

Look out for my CD album, "Holding Hands" on Amazon and Itunes at the end of 2011/ beginning of 2012!

Teurai Chanakira

Teurai Chanakira
by Bechtel Photography

Quote:

"You need to become the change you want to see." (Mahatma Gandhi)

Bio:

Teurai Chanakira is a Law Graduate, Model, Writer/Blogger, Fashion Editor, Fashion Writer (for Skyhost, Air Zimbabwe in-flight Magazine column called How to wear) and Founder of the Elizabeth Chanakira Cancer Trust in Harare, Zimbabwe. Teurai left Zimbabwe when she was 13 to live in Bonn, Germany with her parents. Since then she has lived and travelled all over the world, including living in the UK for ten years and in Australia since 2008.

Although she always had a passion for fashion and dreams of being a model since a young age, her modelling journey only began in Cairns, Australia in 2009 when she was approached by the owner of a popular local store, Tuba Rose, to model the Autumn/Winter collection. Subsequently, she had her first photo shoot and she was "hooked", but what really drove her was the lack of Aboriginal, Indigenous and other models of colour in the Australia media and indeed of black models in other fashion industries worldwide.

Her modelling career catapulted and she accomplished several titles, including being the September 2009 Female Winner in Beautiful People Magazine online; she became the inaugural Brand Ambassador for the clothing label, Authentic Fashion Renaissance; was the face of the Zimbabwean International Music Awards 2010, was in the Top 100 of Naomi Campbell's Global Model Search, out of 8,000 entries worldwide; was named Top Inaugural Model on Zimbo Jam (a Zimbabwean online Arts & Cultural website) and in April 2011, was the first African Finalist ever in the Miss Fashion Australia Awards 2011, since its inception.

Teurai holds a Bachelor of Laws and a Master of Laws from the University of Birmingham, UK and the University of Wolverhampton, UK respectively. She studied Law because she had a deep desire to help those who face injustices. Throughout her legal studies, she rediscovered her childhood love of writing and as she gained global media exposure due to her modelling, she started a blog where she writes about social issues at _www.teuraimodel.com_; subsequently created her own modelling website at _www.teurai.com_ and was then offered a position as a Columnist for the Zimbo Jam (with her own column, "Teurai's Lists"); as a Fashion Editor for the AfriQan Times Australia and as the Fashion Blogger for Afrimarque Events, Australia.

After a seven-year battle with Cancer, Teurai's mother passed away in December 2010. It was then that Teurai founded the Elizabeth Chanakira Cancer Trust (ECCT) in Harare, Zimbabwe. The ECCT is the first organisation of its kind in Zimbabwe as it provides monetary support to poverty-stricken Zimbabwean cancer patients and has a focus on Natural Health & Fitness to reduce the risk of cancer. It will also provide other support such as donations of cancer-related drugs, counselling etc.

How were you as a child—was there anything outstanding about your personality?

Looking back, all the things I loved as a child tie in PRECISELY with all my passions in the present day. I was very quiet, painfully shy, loved to laugh, lived in my own imaginary world, was an avid reader, particularly books by Enid Blyton, Stephen King and I had a children's Bible with beautiful, colourful pictures, which I read over and over again. I remember that my parents flooded me with books from a very early age and so in school, I excelled at essay writing, spelling and was always top of my English class from primary school and throughout high school.

I was very active and so from a tender age, I was always riding my bike around the neighbourhood. I was a good swimmer and was in the Tennis and Hockey school teams. By the time I started university, I rode a bike to classes; jogged and went to the gym regularly. Therein stems my love of Natural Health & Fitness and how I have made it one of the fundamental objectives of the Elizabeth Chanakira Cancer Trust.

I also enjoyed playing "dress-ups" and I remember how, when my friends came over to visit, my older sister would put on "a fashion show" for us, sometimes dressing up in mismatched outfits, so we could burst out in fits of giggles.

Do you remember when you first realised your talent?

As a Law student, (when I finally got serious in my second year lol), I obtained top marks for my writing in exams and assignments. When I studied a Law conversion course in Australia from 2008-2010, I did voluntary work as a Legal Editor for Presidian Legal Publications, where I edited statute books and texts used in Law schools and by practitioners such as lawyers and judges. My editing was of such a high standard that I was offered a paid role. I also obtained a Distinction average for my Australian Law degree.

It's strange that I never really "connected the dots" in terms of realising that I was meant to be a Writer until earlier this year, when one day I suddenly thought, "oh my goodness, this is why I was so good in my English classes and in Law assignments . . . I was meant to do this!" You see, throughout my legal studies, I was never happy. To be honest, I was quite depressed and always wondered why. I just felt like I was standing in some sort of queue in society's factory: where you wait to go to university, get your degree, get a graduate job, get married, have kids and pay off your mortgage.

When I decided to study Law, it was a mixture of my passion for fighting for injustices; discouragement from my parents of what I really wanted to do; mixed with what I felt they and society expected me to do.

All the "nothing" I felt within me all those years finally began to dissolve when I became a model, whose primary purpose is to inspire and empower women of colour to *never* think less of themselves; when I started writing about the issues that affect myself and society without fighting invisible 'red tape' and the bureaucracy that often surrounds lawyers and writing about all the positive, inspirational people I meet.

So, to answer the question, I didn't realise "a talent" per se, I just finally feel alive in what I do and that's all I know!

Who/what was your inspiration?

I have many inspirations. The first one is God because I believe that God and what He created all around me—other people and nature, have inspired me to be who I am today. My main inspiration for pushing to be a model in the tough Australian modelling industry is the passion I have for wanting to see more people of colour, on an international level, on billboards, on TV etc. Yes, we have models like Alek Wek, Tyra

Banks etc but they are simply not enough compared to the majority of white models who we see. Even such prominent models complain at how there is still a lack of colour in the industry and I don't think it is any sort of 'complex' that we have as people of colour, it's just reality.

And who inspires my writing? So many things, but most importantly—people: inspirational, positive, people and personal experiences that I go through, that others go through too and which I want to share with the world; so that we can all find one voice, encourage and empower each other.

Was there anyone who noticed your special talent, did you get any moral support?

The people I work with, primarily photographers, the teams from the magazines and the blog that I write for, teach me so much and we give each other endless moral support, as we are like-minded. Many of them have become good friends.

Also, from the time that I started modelling and subsequently writing, my best friend Maria Magembe and her husband, Robert, have always supported me in my chosen career paths. Furthermore, my sister, Eden Chiuslekuda, is someone who never falters in her support of what I do. I have so many other people who are too many to mention here, who have supported me, including people I haven't met who send me encouraging emails and/or messages on Facebook.

Last, but by no means least, I get moral support from the Power higher than us. Being a creative is not easy because you often do not have evidence about the certainty of the realization of your dreams. I go on 'gut instinct'—that unfaltering 'feeling' that my path is going to work out for me, even when no one can see it . . . and that 'gut instinct' is God telling me to just . . . trust.

How did people react to you when they noticed you were different—were you understood?

Many people did not understand me when they noticed I was different i.e. that I was a Creative, as opposed to "the Commercial Lawyer" that they would have expected me to be. This was particularly hard for my parents, who are Academics and come from a generation where Creative Artists were not seen as really 'working', using their brains or able to make a living from their work.

I remember my late mother trying her best to understand and accept my path, often remarking how beautiful I looked in certain magazines, but I have to admit that deep down I knew she would have preferred me to be "the Commercial Lawyer", but only

because she loved me (and still does in her spirit form) and wants what she sees as best for me—I accept that. As for my father, I know he would love me to be the Commercial Lawyer he boasts that I am, but alas, I cannot be that which I am not destined to be. Many of my other family and friends still do not understand what I do and my purpose, but I have learnt the importance of just being Teurai and accepting that not everyone can understand me.

Being Zimbabwean, what were/ are expectations towards you as a female artist/creative being?

As a female Zimbabwean creative, I think that sometimes we are expected not to soar very high, particularly in the Zimbabwean Creative industry, which is still blossoming.

What I have found commonplace as a model, is that when you are in a male-dominated space, there is a tendency to initiate inappropriate topics or divert discussion to areas that are nothing to do with your work, such as queries regarding your relationship status. This arguably ties in with the stereotype of models not having any brains and being promiscuous.

There needs to be a realisation that modelling is also work. You don't need to look very far to see pictures of people on our food cartons, book covers, shop windows, anywhere . . . to realise the power of global marketing and how we live our lives around it—sometimes being influenced by the smiling face we see, to test out a product. And that's just a fraction of what models can do or contribute. To make it as a model in today's world, you have to be well-rounded, and not just a pretty face . . . indeed that can very well be the last of your attributes.

Whilst living in Harare in 2011 and experiencing the Zimbabwean Fashion Industry, I have noticed that models are not regarded in a very respectful manner, often seen as women with no brains and loose morals. This is disappointing. I think there is still a lot that the Zimbabwean Industry can learn from industries around the world, so that models are given more training, the chance to interact with and share knowledge with photographers and others in the industry more, for example, by having a site such as Model Mayhem (*www.modelmayhem.com*) tailored specifically for people in the Zimbabwean Fashion Industry; broader opportunities and respect as people.

What path did you take to follow your vision?

My path was not the conventional path. In this digital world, I owe a large chunk of my career to the internet, to social sites such as Facebook. Even though I am also with Boss modelling agency, Melbourne, I am more of a Freelance Model, meaning that I source my own assignments and people approach me for work. Being with an agency in Australia has its own challenges, including often being told you will probably not get much work as a model of colour, being told to have a specific hairstyle so you can get more work, etc. So you either buy into that or forge your own path . . . I choose the latter.

When I first started out, I joined a website called Model Mayhem (*www.modelmayhem.com*), where you can network with photographers, designers, makeup artists, etc. There is the opportunity to get free shoots, in which the model and photographer 'pay' each other by TFP (Time For Print) i.e. an exchange of each other's time. I was able to build my portfolio in this way as I was offered shoots by many professional photographers, particularly in a market where there were not many models of colour. I am a petite model, being 5' 6" in height, but I have been given the ability to simply transform in pictures. I got many ongoing referrals after shoots and it just continued from there. However, I now charge for my shoots due to my experience.

Whenever I did a shoot, I posted a few photos on Facebook and soon, people started noticing my talent and creativity as a model. I 'added' friends on Facebook and was 'added' by many people in the Entertainment, Fashion, Media and other related industries. I learnt the value of marketing on Facebook, including basic etiquette, such as introducing myself to people in related industries, directing them to my website and briefly explaining what I do and *why*. I think the latter is very important because it shows my heart and that I'm not just a title—'Model, Writer,' etc. If you are genuine, soon enough, it will show.

From then on, offers for work started coming in and I have built a strong network of friends and contacts who I work with, ask advice from and visa versa, recommend to others, etc. Never underestimate the value of networking and building solid, respectful, professional, relationships. I also started a separate Facebook Model page under 'Teurai Chanakira Model'.

As I gained more exposure in the media as a model, I started my other passion—writing—and started a blog at *www.teuraimodel.com*. Whenever I blog, I also post it to my Facebook pages and this helps Teurai as a brand to develop further. The posting of my blog got me noticed by Zimbo Jam, AfriQan Times Australia and the event company, Afrimarque—all of whom I now write for.

Another very important issue which many models overlook is the importance of working well with people—agents, photographers, designers, *anyone* you are working with on location, including waitresses, cleaners etc. Thank them; be appreciative for everyone's time and effort as it all contributes to the final outcome, that picture that may be seen worldwide. How you treat and interact with others is very influential in whether you will be booked for more work. No matter whether you become a Supermodel, *everyone* deserves respect and there is no time for whining, being mean or complaining that you don't like the outfit etc . . . do your job, you are blessed to be there and to be doing something you love.

What is it that you would like to accomplish/ have accomplished (for yourself or anyone) with your creative talent?

I would like to continue to experience positive growth within my spirit and to continue to follow 'that feeling', which has led me through the darkest hours to the light and is walking me towards even brighter days, which I can see just over yonder. I would like to continue being inspired by and inspiring others and spreading as much positivity as I can in my personal and professional relationships.

Within the next five years, I will be happy to realise my dreams of the Elizabeth Chanakira Cancer Trust Centre in Harare, its registration outside of Zimbabwe and the establishment of businesses which will support the ECCT and witness the growth in value of Teurai as a brand.

What do you think could be done to empower creative children (in Zimbabwe)?

As a people, we need to start accepting creativity as an important part of self. We should recognise that some children are meant to be creatives, others will want to follow their dreams of being a Lawyer, Doctor, Teacher etc, but crushing the former, will only breed a future generation that feels repressed in some way and so the cycle will continue. Let children dream and follow their own paths! Stop dreaming for them.

I am very much in favour of "Montessori-type" schools in Zimbabwe, where the creativity in children is nurtured and encouraged. Even if we don't have such schools, it would be wonderful if creativity could be nurtured in *all* Zimbabwean schools.

Students should also be taught how to be financially smart in the Creative Industry as many adults struggle now (they were never told how to be!) and more importantly, to respect the work of those who follow such a career path. I think that the more respect artists gain from us as a nation, the more likely it is that they will start being adequately socially and financially attributed for their art forms in the Zimbabwean market.

What message do you have for creative women who feel they have no one to turn to?

Sometimes it may seem like nothing is working, that you are stuck in a rut, but just *push* yourself to believe and dream. Listen to your heart, to your spirit—when you have 'that feeling', the feeling that this is your calling, it's usually right. God gave us instincts for a reason, it's Him talking to us—listen to and trust Him. Even when no one understands or supports you, just focus and visualise your goals—eventually something will happen; someone will call; you will think to call someone you had never thought of before—you will attract situations into your life. Surround yourself with like-minded people, read positive books, find out if there are any events which showcase your art form, attend them and network like your life depended on it. Even if you are shy, most people there are probably feeling just the way you are. Don't stop dreaming . . . never ever stop dreaming.

Teurai's website: www.teurai.com

Teurai's blog: www.teuraimodel. com

Elizabeth Chanakira Cancer Trust: www.elizabethchanakira.org

Facebook : 'Teurai Chanakira Model' http://www.facebook.com/ photo.php?fbid=1015013655716 5492&set=a.1015027789598049 2.560197.868825491&type=1#!/ pages/TEURAI-CHANAKIRA-MODEL/108935135796129

Wizzy Mangoma

Wizzy Mangoma
by Picture Boy Fresh

Quote:

To be able to make it hard in LIFE, you should be willing to walk on a road never walked by anyone before (Wizzy)

Bio:

Wizzy Mangoma is a performing artist, author of the poetry book, "Moment Treasures" and the children's book "Manjanja—The Shining Red Fruit". She is a Spoken Word Artist, Screenplay Writer, Story Teller Dancer/Choreographer, Actress, Model, Designer—(graphics, costumes and accessories), Event Coordinator and Motivational Speaker. Besides travelling with her own group, "Titambe", Wizzy travelled and performed in various groups and projects ranging from United African Ballet Of Denmark to television series.

Besides performing arts, Wizzy worked as a graphic designer for an advertising agency in Denmark. She also taught at the Rhythmic Evening School in Copenhagen and participated in cultural festivals all over Europe. She featured in several magazines, has been a host and judge for fashion shows, as well as beauty pageants. Wizzy has worked with children from all backgrounds, including children with special needs. She has participated as a volunteer mentor and a chairperson for a charity organisation, "United Way". She has been an Area Marketing Director coordinating entertainment events as well as community charity campaigns such as Breast Cancer, Operation Smile (for children born with cleft) and D.A.R.E (Drug Abuse Resistance Education). Her poem, "Tear Drop", won Editor's Choice Award. She has written songs (poems) for a few fellow artists.

Wizzy is always creating. She has written numerous scripts for theaters etc. And, has a script ready for a movie based in Zimbabwe, which she hopes to be filmed sometime in the near future. She also makes inspirational greeting cards. Her passion is to help motivate and inspire, with emphasis on women empowerment and youth mentoring.

She has set up a group called Wizzy's Lounge where people with creative gifts (and those who believe in supporting others) from all angles of the globe can interact and share their thoughts, work, events, ideas and concerns.

How were you as a child—was there anything outstanding about your personality?

I am told that when I was around two years old, after eating dinner, I would just get up and have family members sing for me as I danced. I was known to have a voice for others, to be curious and inquisitive. I always had so many abstract questions in my head. And if I didn't get answers to those questions, I would not relax or sleep well until I got them. I would not let things pass me by. If I saw someone unhappy or being treated unfairly, I made it my duty to do something about it. I had this great passion for playing with clay and I made all kinds of figures. The feeling of soft clay through my fingers is something I found soothing back then. It took me to a peaceful place. I was a happy dreamer.

Do you remember when you first realised your talent?

There are so many things we do as children without thinking much about it. I made my own dolls (with all kinds of materials which I got from my late grandmother). I enjoyed the fact that I could really make such beautiful objects, as well as play with them. My late grandmother taught me how to make little dresses for them and I was so fond of doing so. At school, I always had this glow whenever it was time for Arts & Crafts, as well as Drama. So I can say that, it was in me and I just followed that good feeling I got whenever I created something. While other children talked about being Doctors, Nurses, Teachers etc, I remember talking about wanting to be a Dancer, Designer and an Actress.

Who/what was your inspiration?

Moving around to many different places during childhood play a big role in my life when it comes to my inspiration. Wherever we moved, I met so many different people with cultures and different mind frames. I made many friends who had different types of creative sides to them. We would share ideas or make different things and give them to each other as gifts. This brought so much coulour to my life.

One of my inspirations was my late grandmother. She was one great entrepreneur. She made clothes on her Singer sewing machine and travelled to some villages to sell them. She did not mind me sitting besides her while she did her sewing. She would let me do the threading. Sometimes if she was in the best of moods, she would let me do the cutting. My late grandmother always had this great passion for gardening. I remember her winning a first prize for best and well-maintained yard in her town.

My mother was also another inspiration. She has always been a fashionable, unique individual who knew what she was worth. As far as I remember, she has always been a working mother who always carried a positive smile when she got home from work. As children, whenever we went to her work place, we would see our mother with such radiance because of how much she loved doing her job. After work, she had time to make sure we were well taken care of. Besides working, she had many activities such as counselling people in her community and taking care of maintaining the church with other women of the congregation. She has always participated in church as a Choir Mistress and has always knitted by hand (from complicated pattern books), taking orders from people all over the country.

My family, including my uncles and aunts were such wonderful people to be around. Whenever there was any form of entertainment in our town, the whole family would go together. Also, during weekends at home, we would gather around and be told folk stories or we would listen to Motown, Reggae, African music and dance around.

At Arcturus mine (where I spend some few years of my childhood), there were all kinds of cultural dances, which were held every weekend, which I would not miss for anything. During the week I would follow my Tonga, Chewa and Nyanja friends to their "Chimutare" ladies dance practices. I was allowed to practice with them, but could not dance in the actual show because I did not belong to their tribes. Just being part of something that magnificent was something I looked forward to every week.

Because of one my wonderful uncles (—May his soul rest in peace), I got to meet a lot of musicians like The Wailers, Aswad, King Sounds and the Israelites as well as Misty in Roots. I got to learn a lot from Misty in Roots when I stayed in London with the lead singer and his family. Misty in Roots took me to their studio and to places where they performed. I got to learn about discipline on tour and many things from them. They were always cheerful, calm and collected. And, when they were on stage, they really gave all the energy they had in them. As they performed, I would look and admire each and every band member. Each and every one of them was so unique and yet they delivered the music as ONE.

One other great inspiration was my third grade teacher (who had so much love for theater), listening to stories read on Radio Two and listening to some of our local musicians.

Was there anyone who noticed your special talent, did you get any moral support?

My mother and my family noticed my talent. They gave me all the support a person could need. My mother would teach me how to knit (but my sister mastered that art better) and she would ask me what I really wanted to do in life. When I brought artwork, which I made in school, she always had so many positive comments. Once when I had to enter an artwork competition, my mother encouraged me in every way possible. I made wax batik of an Egyptian bird. I was one of the winners and my artwork was sent to England to be placed in an art gallery.

After school, my mother sent me to England to pursue my dream in designing. When I got back home, she had a private designer "Creed Katsande" (who had just returned to Zimbabwe after many years in the UK) give me private classes. Creed gave me so many tools to prepare me for the world, "The Jungle". I also did some fashion shows with her back then. Most of my teachers noticed something special about me. I was always chosen to represent for my classes, in subjects like Sewing, Drama, Poetry Recital, or Public Speaking.

How did people react to you when they noticed you were different—were you understood?

I think some people have problems understanding the passion that lies inside an artist. Whenever I told some people what my dreams were, some would look at me as if I was just plain crazy and wasting time. A few did tell me I was crazy. Some parents would compare me to their children and they would usually suggest I get a real job. My vision was not good enough for some but at the same time, there were people who believed in me, people who encouraged me to keep going strong. I knew my family was behind me, which was enough fuel for me to keep me going. My family and a few friends knew I was different and very determined. They did not judge me; they motivated me to follow my passion.

Being Zimbabwean, what were/ are expectations towards you as a female artist/creative being?

It is hard to say since I have lived away from Zimbabwe for so long. Since way back, a lot of men have been in the limelight more than women. I wish I could hear how other female artists of all time have managed through all these years. At the same time, regardless of gender, there are struggles, which come with an artistic package. I think many people are comfortable around someone who has a so-called "normal career", someone who works in an office. And, as an artist you really have to be "up there" with some popular names to be considered an artist. I think in many places, if I were to say I am a doctor or something else, I would probably be appreciated more. Being an artist is like being the last in line. But, at the same time, this never stops me from doing what I do. I touch people globally and that is what really counts. From what I see now, a lot more female artists have emerged in Zimbabwe. And they are being embraced with a positive attitude.

What path did you take to follow your vision?

To me it is all about hard work and determination. I think sometimes, to get to any place; one has to work hard to get there. We all know that nothing comes easy in life. At the same time, I think being a creative person makes you work twice as much since some of what we do can be taken as a hobby, depending on where one is located. I was blessed enough to have embraced my unique personality at an early age. This made it easy for me to go out there and get what I wanted. We did not have

Internet back then, so everything was word of mouth or you would go everywhere in person to market yourself. I was in a magazine and in fashion shows for different unique trend shops in Zimbabwe.

Denmark embraced diversity at the time that I moved there, which was a positive thing and a big boost for me. I joined the Artists Union, which gave artists a lot of recognition. I was one of the few Africans in Denmark back then, so I had to work very hard on finding which path to take. My focus was to show a positive image of Africa while developing myself.

As I went to school and worked all day, I had to find a few hours to network with different people to get an understanding of how things worked in the country. I networked with different photographers and had many photo shoots. I also got an agent who got me some commercial and filming jobs. My first years in a Danish school, I took Film and Photography classes and I also did a few fashion shows. This gave me confidence to start my own fashion shows with an ethnic touch to them. This was embraced with such warmth.

During weekends I travelled with an African Dance Group, "Calabash". I made sure that I was always there for practice in order to learn dances from different parts of Africa. The founder of the group was like a father to us. Whenever he saw strength in someone, he would motivate the person more and more by giving that person a leading role. He gave me so many opportunities, which led to me getting all kinds of leadership training offered by the government, as well as representing Calabash on television and in newspapers. I designed some of the costumes for the group, as well as arranging some of the trips. United African Ballet of Denmark hired me, and we performed with many professional actors from the Royal Theatre. I also participated in cultural festivals.

During all this, I was also working as a Graphic Designer for an Advertising bureau. I am not a person who would sit in an office and do one job. I made some clothes including crotchet bikinis and had a Street Wear Shop sell them. I later on gave up the graphic designing job and focused on acting in TV series, doing commercials etc. I also had the opportunity to travel doing theatre and music with another group of well-known musicians in Denmark.

The whole experience gave me so much strength that I started my own theatre, "Titambe". We travelled to places doing story telling through theatre, music and dance. I got to know so much about theatre management on this journey.

When it comes to writing, I always had it in me. I kept writing and reading my poetry to my friends by candlelight. I joined a writers' group and participated in writers' seminars (mainly script writing) to develop more skills. I recorded some of my poetry and posted them on a MySpace page. The feedback I got from people always motivated me to do more. I had Speech classes in college and was elected one of the motivational speakers for the college. I also had a poetry and book club (with friends from college) where we met every Friday to keep each other going. I kept writing and compiling my work until I was ready to get published.

One great networking place I am grateful for is Facebook. We are able to make this book project because Facebook gave us an opportunity to meet wonderful creative women. I am where I am today because of these paths which I took. I would not trade any of my experiences for anything.

What is it that you would like to accomplish/ have accomplished (for yourself or anyone) with your creative talent?

Whatever I do, I put my whole soul in it and let the rest follow. I feel accomplished when I see my finished product right in front of me. Just being able to give the world what I have inside my soul and seeing the world smile, is an accomplishment on its own. The fact that someone out there acknowledges my work, someone out there is touched, someone out there is inspired, makes me feel complete. And it gives me a reason to keep on doing more. As long as I can help someone get up in the morning feeling motivated just from reading some of my work, is a reward to me. I would like people to be able to feel my heart and believe in themselves as they follow their passion. I just want to keep doing what I do best and grow. And hope that all the work that I do will have a great impact on others.

What do you think could be done to empower creative children (in Zimbabwe)?

Children need encouragement to reach their fullest potential possible. First of all, it has to start from home. Children thrive from love and support from their family members. Parents can always utilize the time they spend with their children at home to really see their inner strength. They don't have to leave everything to the schoolteachers to see certain signals, which may indicate how creative a child is. They should pay attention and not take any of their children's artwork for granted. Some creative children may seem like dreamers in class. It does not mean they are not good or smart students. It is just because they may find other subjects very challenging.

Schools should have classes designed for children like that to help them accelerate in class.

Teachers should also get more education, which focuses on what to look for in a creative child. This really gives creative children a special feeling of being appreciated. One great way to empower creative children is through the sale of their artwork and more exposure. They need to go out and experience all sorts of art events/festivals. Mentorship programs should be implemented (if they don't already exist) in schools and communities to provide a way forward for these children.

What message do you have for creative women who feel they have no one to turn to?

Everything has its time, no matter how hard it may seem. Never give up on yourself. Things come through determination, passion and hard work. Follow your heart and be true to yourself. Try NOT to surround yourself with negative people because they can only bring you down. Network with people who share the same passion. Talk to someone (with a positive outlook to life) about your passion. There is someone out there ready to listen, ready to help you take the path and maybe ready to work with you. Market yourself because gone are the days when people did everything for someone. You are your own product and who best can sell your product but YOURSELF.

For Wizzy's spoken word music http://www.myspace.com/wizzyma

Or http://soundcloud.com/ wizzymangoma

For poetry book "Moment Treasures" go to www.Amazon.com

For the Children Book Manjanja—The Shining Red Fruit—go to www. Amazon.com

Facebook: search for 'Wizzy Mangoma'

You are also welcome to join Wizzy's Lounge on facebook

www.ingramcontent.com/pod-product-compliance
Lightning Source LLC
Chambersburg PA
CBHW031238280526
45784CB00004B/1621